RUN TO WIN
"Love and Sacrifice"

By

Charlie Capozzoli

Published by CJC Publishing Group

Edition: 10 9 8 7 6 5 4 3   SAN: 850–5438

Library of Congress Control Number: 2007909778

ISBN-13: 978-0-9779039-8-6
ISBN-10: 0-9779039-8-2

Printed and Bound in Ann Arbor, MI
        United States of America.
This Book is printed on Acid Free Paper

TABLE OF CONTENTS

INTRODUCTION...V

CHAPTER 1 - The Family...1

CHAPTER 2 - Growing Up In College Point. 10

CHAPTER 3 – Grandpa..14

CHAPTER 4 - Living In Flushing..20

CHAPTER 5 - Our Faith...25

CHAPTER 6 - Bayside High School Days............................29

CHAPTER 7 - Hard Work, Aches, Pain and Angels.............33

CHAPTER 8 - So Long Bayside, Hello Georgetown.............46

CHAPTER 9 - Junior Year At Georgetown..........................73

CHAPTER 10 - XV Olympiad, Helsinki, Finland..................79

CHAPTER 11 - Capozzoli Versus Pirie In England..............97

CHAPTER 12 - Senior Year At Georgetown.......................103

CHAPTER 13 - Capozzoli Beats Ashenfelter......................118

CHAPTER 14 - Illness Set-Back, But Never Give Up...........129

CHAPTER 15 - Capozzoli Runs 4:07.8 mile........................131

CHAPTER 16 - Drake Relays, Des Moines, Iowa
                1952 and 1953...............................137

CHAPTER 17 - California, Here We Come................144

CHAPTER 18 - Goodbye Georgetown.....................161

CHAPTER 19 - Last Trip To Germany....................173

CHAPTER 20 - Last Trip To Italy.........................176

CHAPTER 21 - Home From Europe.......................181

CHAPTER 22 - The Sullivan Award
                           and The Kevilles....................189

CHAPTER 23 - Run For Fun..............................191

CHAPTER 24 - My Final Race, Yours Too............... 193
                   Georgetown Trophy Room..............195
                   Letters of Honor.....................205
                   Our Wedding Day....................210
                   Capozzoli Children..................216
                   John's Three Miracles................219
                   My Parents..........................232
                   My Adopted Family, Semper Fi........237

Introduction

I, the author of "Run to Win," "Love and Sacrifice," dedicate this true story of my youthful life to my parents, brother, sister, grandfather, uncle mike, aunts, uncles, cousins, and friends who took an interest in my life as "a young boy who had a dream." They encouraged me to do my best in life. Without their "Love," it would not have been possible to achieve the goals that I set out to do.

My greatest joy came later in life when meeting my wife, Donna, and her giving birth to our four precious children, John, Donna Marie, Janine, and Joseph... Sadly, Donna passed away Dec. 21st, 2001, followed by our first-born child, John, on Sept. 2nd, 2005. This story is likewise dedicated to them, our children, their spouses, and our "18 grandchildren."

Vanity could be a reason for writing this. However, the main purpose is for my children, their spouses, and their children (our grandchildren) to have something to look back on. May they always remember that in life "it's love that really matters!" It is so important to tell one another that "I love you!" It can change ones' life!

Most of all, I thank our God for His love and the never ending gifts that He gives us.

Love and God bless,

Charlie

Mom and Dad

Louie, Mom, Marion, Dad and Charlie (me)

Chapter 1
"The Family"

This is about the life of a seventy-four year old man. It seems like only yesterday when I was a young boy. The years go by so very fast in our lifetime! Therefore, each day of our lives is extremely important that not one minute should be wasted.

"Run to win—love and sacrifice," have many meanings which can be expressed in different ways, such as, " Never give up—Do your best—Nothing is impossible—Don't let anyone tell you what you can't do—It's love that really matters!" This goes on, on, and on. As this brief story of my childhood is told, there will be incidents relating to the above to illustrate how you can change your life.

My parents were Americans of Italian descent, both born in New York City. My father, Joseph Capozzoli, went to Italy at the age of two with his mother, a grandmother whom I never had the privilege of meeting. At the age of seventeen, my father returned to America to begin his apprentice as a cobbler, a profession that he pursued for the remainder of his life. He met his lovely wife, Tanella Riccio, in New York. She was the love of his life. Dad passed away at the age of seventy. Mom lived until ninety.

My father dedicated his life to his family, working six days a week (sometimes seven) in order that his family had comfortable living accommodations, shelter, food, and clothing. My mother devoted her life to her husband and children. They concentrated their lives on each other and their children. It was the family that was of great importance to them "love and sacrifice!"

While World War11 was going on full force, my brother, Lou, sister Marion, and I never feared it. Our parents gave us their love and a deep sense of security. They were proud Americans, taught us never to hate anyone, not the Germans or the Japanese. The Japanese bombed Pearl Harbor Dec. 7th, 1941, destroying many of our ships, killing our military, as well as our citizens. In spite of this, we had to respect everyone, especially our elders. Never would my parents criticize the President of his decisions pertaining to the war. He declared war on Japan, December 8th, after they bombed Pearl Harbor. At the same time, Hitler was on a rampage to conquer Europe, invading one country after another. Hitler declared war on the United States, December 11th. He killed millions of people in Europe, especially Jews who were mercilessly murdered in gas chambers. We, Americans, lost lots of young men who went to war to protect America and the nations of Europe. They fought proudly for freedom and gave their lives in doing so.

During the war, we did have some frightful moments as sirens sounded (air-raid drills) in the early evenings. It was lights out in the house and sitting in the dark until the drill ended. Even then, the love of our parents made us feel very secure and safe. I did, however, scare everyone.

"Charlie," Mom said, "go into the small hallway room and bring me the tiny lamp so that we can at least have a little light. I'll put a towel over it so the light can't be seen from the outside."

The shades were already drawn. Unable to unplug the lamp, I got a kitchen knife, placed it between the socket and the plug to pry it loose. Boom! I blew out the entire circuit in the house. The knife flew out of my hands (burnt a hole in the knife), and my parents had the biggest scare ever during an air raid drill. This convinced me that I never wanted to be an electrician.

It also frightened our German friends who lived downstairs (we rented the upper level from Mr. Katz). We loved them, and knew they had nothing to do with the war (or blowing out the circuits, Ha! Ha!) They too had come to America for a new life, as many immigrants did, all being proud to live here. Their son, Roland, was my good friend who would come to my aid if some bully picked on me.

Dad had his shoe repair shop in a small town in College Point, New York. He had a black man helping him fix shoes. He allowed two mentally retarded men to visit in the store, remaining at the front counter watching him fix shoes. My brother, Lou, and I, (11 and 8 years old), "the shoe shine boys", had to acknowledge them as we would anyone else. Dad would not tolerate anyone making fun of them. Dad's customers knew his feelings towards people who were not gifted as most of us.

Dad had a thriving business, especially during the war when shoes were rationed. Someone recommended to dad that he should raise his prices.

He refused to do so, saying, "How can I raise prices when the families in College Point have sons in the military, giving their lives to protect us!" Dad was greatly admired for this. He, and the name "Roxy Shoe Repair," won the respect of all. When the G.I.s returned home, one of their important stops was to visit dad, who welcomed them by treating to a drink at the beer bar across the street. Lou and I watched the store. We could see dad across the street and wave to him if needed. They loved him, and he loved them. Lou and I had the privilege of shining their shoes. Dad made sure that their shoes sparkled. How proud we were of these young men. We looked up to them as very special. They beamed proudly to wear the American uniform. Never did they regret that their young lives were interrupted by the war. At an early age, I realized that I would someday volunteer or be drafted in the service after completing high school. It was something all male teenagers expected, unless there were unusual circumstances. I was fortunate not to be drafted, having received college scholarship offers for my running ability, being one of the fastest high school milers in the United States, missing the National High School record by one and seven tenths of a second (see picture on cover). Georgetown University later became my second home for five years, four years in the School of Foreign Service and one year of Law School.

While mom attended to her chores at home (a full time job), dad left early in the morning to open his shoe repair shop. We never did see him until late evenings in time for us to gather around the dinner table. Mom prepared a different meal each day. Of course, pasta was our favorite, especially with the delicious meatballs and salad to go with it. Should any of the neighborhood children ring our doorbell at dinnertime to see if Lou and I could go out to play, they knew it was an immediate invitation to join us.

"Please have dinner with us," my parents would welcome them.

They happily did! Before eating our dinner, it was my job to bring a platter of spaghetti and meatballs to our neighbors on the right and left side of us for them to enjoy. I tried to keep the conversation short with them, so that I could hurry home to eat mine.

Dinnertime was always a great treat for us. It was a time to carry on conversations, listening to my parent's childhood, how they met and fell in love. My grandfather also lived with us (the only grandparent alive whom we ever knew). Being born in Italy, grandpa would tell us about his childhood. Sometimes we couldn't understand him, but listened attentively anyway. During the dinner, dad and grandpa enjoyed a hearty bottle of red wine. My job was to have the wine on the table before dad entered home. I had good hearing then and knew when he arrived by the sound of his car pulling in the driveway. Once dinner was over, it was time for everyone to do what they wanted. It was time for dad and grandpa to relax, to listen to the radio in the living room, while mom cleaned the kitchen and washed the dishes. I never did see dad wash a dish or mom repair shoes! Each knew their duties and responsibilities. We children had to do our homework. There was no TV (or computer!) at this time in our lives. We never missed it, for our lives seemed so much better without it. More conversations took place. Our parents made our lives seem so important, listening to what our day was like. Our parents gave us radio time to listen to the "Lone Ranger and Tonto," "Inner Sanctum" and "Dr. Kildare." Ha! Ha! They listened too.

Childhood in those days was not so complicated as it is today. Drugs were unheard of. Sex was never discussed, although we did learn about the birds and the bees in a decent manner. Discipline was expected. Do something wrong, and expect to be reprimanded by dad as soon as he arrived home, even though mom got her few whacks in first. While attending parochial school, dad told the nuns (he repaired their shoes) that they had his permission to spanks us, as long as they told him later, so he could spank us again. We had to stand erect in front of dad at the time of being reprimanded, hands down at our side, and no blocking when the slap (soft blow) approached our face. Dare to block a slap, more would then follow.

On Saturdays, we were allowed to go out to play only after doing chores, such as making our bed, dusting under the dining room table, which was later chopped up for firewood to keep us warm during the cold winter days. My parents later regretted having done this, but it did keep us warm for awhile. Mom was very immaculate in keeping a clean house. You could eat off the floor. One day, she passed by the bathroom while I was brushing my teeth. Mom looked at the toothbrush I was using.

"You're using the tooth brush that I use to clean the woodwork." she said.

We both laughed, although I would have been happy if my teeth came out as white as the woodwork. When playing outside, it was roller skating, baseball, touch football, diamond ball, and stickball. Brooms came in handy as stick ball bats. We played lots of other games requiring running which was my cup of tea, since I was skinny and could run, run, and run. We knew that regardless of what or where we were playing, we had to be home by a certain time for dinner, or else! We had to be within distance to hear dad's shrilling whistle. Our playmates also heard it and advised us, "You better go home!" There was no such thing as telling dad we didn't hear his whistle.

Mom was more concerned that we played sports in which we wouldn't get hurt. That was impossible! Playing touch football in the streets of New York presented possible injuries like being pushed into a neighbor's wall, or knocked down to the pavement. When playing touch football, I went to block a pass and slammed into my opponents open mouth whose tooth pierced my head. I told my brother not to mention this to mom when we got home. Later that night, Lou explained to her what had happened. All hell broke loose! Mom checked my head to see where the tooth had penetrated. To be sure that the tooth was not in my head, she took me to my friend's home late at night to meet with him and his mother to see if her son still had all his teeth in his mouth. He did, but that was the end of playing any kind of football.

Mom was a fabulous cook, having learned as a teenager to care for her father, sister and four brothers. Her mother passed away in her early forties. Fortunately, mom had learned from her how to prepare delicious dinners to satisfy the family. After marriage, mom still prepared dinners for her father, sister, and four unmarried brothers. We lived in grandpa's home upstairs and they downstairs. Once all married, except for Uncle Charles, who volunteered in the army and fought in the battles in Europe, it was dinner for her father, my dad, and us children. Any Italian reading this story will remember waking up on Sunday mornings, smelling the gravy and meatballs cooking for dinner. Mom knew how much we wanted to taste a meatball before going to church. She would give us one or two. Sometimes my brother, Lou, managed to get one extra. Between Lou, our sister, Marion, and me, we ate a good number of meatballs before dinner. Mom made enough to feed an army.

At Sunday dinner, which was around two o'clock in the afternoon, it meant at least two hours sitting around the table. First the pasta was served. Being a skinny little kid, two bowls of pasta was enough. I had to save room for the meatballs, chicken, and salad that would follow. By this time, dad and grandpa were feeling good, having finished a couple of bottles of red wine. Neither my brother, sister, nor I would accept their offer to have a little, at least not until we got older. The finale of the dinner was fruit, nuts, and more stories by my parents and grandpa. After dinner mom would clean up the kitchen, dad and grandpa would find a comfortable chair in the parlor (living room) and doze off. We children went out to play to work up an appetite for leftovers later that evening. This was our Sunday treat! And a treat it was! Cake and coffee was served later in the evening, especially when our Aunts and Uncles stopped by for a visit. It meant more food, more conversation, and more laughter.

Sundays were such beautiful memories in our life. Before dinner, we would listen to the battle of the baritones, Frank Sinatra, Perry Como, Vic Damone, Dick Haymes, and so on. The songs and lyrics were so beautiful and inspirational that they became memorable moments in our youthful lives, daydreaming of the wonderful future that lied ahead, like meeting the girl of my dreams. In the evenings, it was grandpa's turn to listen to opera. My brother and I couldn't understand how anyone could like opera. This caused grandpa to become upset with us. We all laughed about it. It was his turn to enjoy the radio. We had ours earlier in the day. There was only one radio in the house and one bathroom for six people. Therefore, we had to learn to share. Sometimes there were emergencies to use the bathroom, but we still managed with no embarrassing incidents.

All the kings in the world never had it as good as my father. My mother treated him like one. Everyday she prepared a different dinner that he liked. He made no demands, but she knew what pleased him, especially after working twelve or more hours a day. He always retired to a bed that was made up, and awoke in the morning to a clean kitchen. Everything was in order. Dad in turn treated mom as a queen, with the greatest respect, the wife he cherished and the children she bore. It was mom's home. She was in charge. My brother, sister, and I, thought that every home was like ours. There was a hug and a kiss in the morning when we would arise, and the same in the evening before we closed our eyes.

Before marriage, mom was known in town as "beautiful Tanella," with the attractive hair-style and classy dresses. She was sought after by many men. Dad, however, was the victor, himself being handsome, looking somewhat like Rudolph Valentino (actually more handsome). He wooed mom and won her love. Friends of dad's would have given anything to have my mother as their bride, but they couldn't play the mandolin and sing to mom as dad did. Once married, mom's fancy dresses ended up in the closet to be worn on special occasions only. Her daily dress code became an apron and hair net. It was now time to clean house, cook, and raise a family. How proud dad was of her, for she pleased him in every way. Their wedding picture is so beautiful that to this day it is admired by all who see it. We laugh though when told that dad stood on a telephone book covered by mom's wedding gown so that he would look taller than she did.

While living in Mr. Katz's house in College Point on the second floor, we knew all of our neighbors and they knew us. Our Aunts and Uncles lived across the street or around the corner. Therefore, the eyes of loved ones were always watching over us. If you did something wrong, you could expect that mom and dad knew about it by the time we got home. How wonderful it was to visit our Aunts and Uncles within walking distance. The visits included milk, crackers with cream cheese and jelly, and sometimes doughnuts. On the corner of the street where we lived in College Point, there was a beverage stand where we would buy Pepsis and pretzels. Many happy and fun times were spent there with Uncle Mike who was more like a brother than an Uncle, being mom's youngest brother and only a several years older than Lou and I.

Uncle Mike also worked in dad's shoe repair shop fixing shoes. Being very handsome, young beautiful women would bring in their shoes for repair just to see and to talk to him. I fell in love with them and wished that I was more than just the shoeshine-boy. Uncle Mike was like the CEO. In time, now being ten years old, I was allowed to wait on customers and asked what they wanted. Many of the young women wore high heels in those days. I would ask if they would like "lips!"

Dad overheard me one day, and questioned me, "What do you ask?" he said laughingly. "It's lifts, not lips!"

No wonder I got nice smiles from the young ladies.

Once I got too close to the spinning sandpaper machine used to smooth the heels and souls of shoes. My tie got caught! (you had to wear a tie to work in dad's store). The machine pulled my chin right up to it. Uncle Mike immediately grabbed me around the waist, pulled hard to loosen me from the machine and getting severely hurt. If it weren't for Uncle Mike, I would never have had to shave the rest of my life. Uncle Mike had a secret love, a beauty named, Anne, whose father delivered ice and oil in town, "the Pierroes!" We didn't meet her until sometime later. I don't remember her coming to have her shoes repaired. When finally meeting her, it was love at first sight, but she belonged to Uncle Mike. Besides, I was only 12 years old and couldn't think of marriage.

My brother, Lou, and I were the shoeshine boys under the close supervision of dad and Uncle Mike. The mornings in the store started off with a big cup of coffee (half coffee and half milk) with buns for dunking. For lunch, it was cold cuts from the delicatessen next door, followed up later in the afternoon with a chocolate malt, which was the best ever, thick and creamy. Lou and I had lots of fun in the store. My dad often wondered if we came there to work or just to have a good time. It was both! We enjoyed being with dad and Uncle Mike, while at the same time making enough money on tips to buy bow ties and flashy socks, all different colors, like Frank Sinatra wore. This was our reward for hard work. Oh! I forgot when mom would make us lunch every so often. I would bring it to dads' store for us to eat instead of having cold cuts from the deli all the time. It was made of Italian bread, crispy and fresh, sliced down the middle, with fried round steak, onions, and peppers in between. Wow! My taste buds are going crazy as I write this. Dad had a glass or two of red wine to go with it, while Lou and I had a big bottle of Pepsi Cola.

One September day, in 1941, when I was ten years old, mom gave birth to a beautiful baby girl. I hurried home from school so excited to see her that I wet my pants on the way. Uncle Mike was waiting outside the house for me. He too was excited, but didn't wet his pants. We then went upstairs to see my sister. How happy we were! Lou and I now had a sister, named Marion. We called her "Maggie" at times. It was Marion who later in life took care of Lou, as he became handicapped and required care around the clock. Mom and dad were in heaven. I lived three thousand miles away in California. Marion devoted many years of her life caring for Lou until he recently passed away to join mom and dad. Neither complained about their circumstances in life. It was "sacrifice and love" that got them through each day, with joy and laughter along the way. I have had the good fortune of knowing two saints, Lou and Marion.

"As a child, I remember mom and dad, the fun, the good times and the sad, the love they gave, the sacrifices made, I will always remember mom and dad."

Chapter 2
"Growing up in College Point."

Marion, Lou and Charlie

College Point was a very quaint town, a suburb of New York City. It was only several miles to La Guardia airport and another twenty minute drive to the heart of the city. Many immigrants came and settled there, mostly Italians, Germans and Jews. We all got along together and never paid attention to ethnic differences. We were Americans.

As mentioned in chapter 1, my father had his shoe repair shop in town. Next door was a drug store. Across the street a beer bar. Next to it a Greek restaurant where I would go for a delicious pizza and a large Pepsi for 25 cents. There was a butcher shop, a German bakery, and many "mom & pop" type stores where one could do all their shopping. (As of several years ago, the town council was and still is against having a Wal-Mart). There was a movie theater, the only one in town. Lou and I would go there for fifteen cents, with the biggest bag of potato chips one could buy at Woolworths for a nickel. In front of each store, built in the sidewalk, was a holder for the American flag. All stores would put out the American flag on special occasions. Lou and I had the job of putting the flag out for dad. The pole was about eight feet high. Dad kept it in the back of his store. The parade would then go by with saxophones, clarinets, trumpets, bugles, and drums blaring away, while veterans marched proudly wearing their medals. What a thrill it was for everyone to see.

Lou and I now wanted to play an instrument so that we too could someday march in the parade. Lou took saxophone and clarinet lessons. I joined the local militia so that I could learn to play any kind of instrument and wear their fancy uniform. When the band director gave me the tuba, which was bigger than I, I had a change of heart. I then thought of being a singer like Frank Sinatra or Perry Como. My dad, being a singer himself in his teens,

"Sing the scale, you know, do, re, mi," he said to me. After listening, he politely said, "You aren't ready yet."

Guess he had something else in store for me, but he still arranged for me to go with two teenage girl members of Perry Como's fan club to meet him. We attended his birthday party after his supper club performance. Wow! Perry Como offered me by name a piece of his birthday cake. However, little did I know that my athletic ability, being able to run, run, and run, would be in my dad's thoughtful mind. He always said I had the chest of an athlete when I was born. At an early age, like ten years old, he would hand me a quarter and tell me to "run to the store" to buy him a pack of Lucky Strikes. I didn't know until years later that he would time me to see how fast I'd go. Did he know that the day would come when I would run in the Olympic games, representing the United States of America, and be the American three mile run champion and record holder by the age of twenty-one?

My brother, Lou, wasn't able to run as most children could. My parents recognized this and became greatly concerned, taking him from doctor to doctor, to see why he wasn't agile as I was. The doctors couldn't figure it out and recommended special treatments, like calisthenics. They tried this, but Louie just couldn't do the exercise. Guess that's why mom and dad had a German professor come to the house to teach him how to play the saxophone and clarinet. It was something he did well and enjoyed, later joining a band and playing at local dances. Loving Louie as I did, we watched over each other. He was three years older than I was. In spite of his handicap, he handled himself well in a fistfight, although I worried knowing that his legs couldn't hold up. My dad and Uncle Mike taught us how to fist-fight. You had to learn to in New York. When Louie was fist-fighting this kid who picked on him, I went across the street where there was a bushel of ripe tomatoes in front of our neighbor's home. I picked up a big tomato and threw it at the kid Louie was fighting. It hit him on the side of his face, a perfect shot! He then looked at me, stopped fighting my brother, and chased after me. I ran around my Aunt and Uncle's home yelling, "Aunt Lena, Uncle Carmen, help!"

Around and around their home I ran (marathon?) until he finally gave up the chase. After many years of going from doctor to doctor, it was determined that Louie had a mild touch of Polio when younger and nothing could now be done.

Did you ever see meatballs rolling in dirt? During summertime, our families would picnic at Alley Pond Park. Each family would bring food. Some would bring coffee, donuts, bacon and eggs. Another family would bring buns, sauerkraut, hot dogs, hamburgers and onions, to be cooked on the grills. Another would bring watermelon, fruit, and nuts. Another dessert. Every family brought their beer, wine, and soda for the kids. Mom made the gravy and meatballs. Everyone loved mom's meatballs and gravy. When we arrived at the picnic grounds, like 7:00 am, mom asked me to carry the pot of gravy with the meatballs. Excited to get to the picnic table, besides the pot being heavy, I tripped on a tree stump. The pot flew out of my hands! The gravy and meatballs went rolling along the ground. Suddenly, all these Italian eyes were looking at me in amazement (or was it anger?) I began to cry, (had to do something to keep from getting killed). My parents, Aunts, Uncles, and cousins, then came to me.

"Don't cry, Charlie," they said, "we have lots of other food with us."

The day turned out to be a joyful one. My dropping the meatballs went down in family history, never to be forgotten, but forgiven?

There were some sad moments in our youthful lives, one being Louie's problem, the other being the death of my three year old cousin, Marie, whom I adored. I was five years old at the time, but old enough to feel this terrible tragedy. She had diphtheria, a contagious disease causing inflammation of the heart and nervous system. Being contagious, cautious steps had to be taken to prevent it from spreading to her sisters, Lou, and I. Our families were close and always together. This was a most difficult time in our lives, especially for Aunt Lena and Uncle Carmen. Mom stored Marie's clothes in a small spare room in grandpa's home. Without anyone knowing it, I would go into this room, open the drawer where her clothes were and smell them, a beautiful fragrance that reminded me of someone I loved so much. The tears now roll down my face as they did then. How precious she was.

"Although we are now far apart, their love lingers on in my heart, the love they gave, the sacrifices made; I will always remember mom and dad. Marie too!"

Chapter 3
Grandpa

GRANDPA AND HIS FOUR SONS

LEFT TO RIGHT: UNCLE TONY, UNCLE BILL, GRANDPA, UNCLE CHARLES, UNCLE MIKE
(GRANDPA RULED WITH AN IRON HAND. THEY LOVED AND RESPECTED HIM FOR IT)

Grandpa was born in Italy. Like many other immigrants, he came to America for better opportunities. While he couldn't read or write English fluently, besides having a slight problem enunciating, he still managed to be successful, owning several homes in the early twenties. Mom always said that grandpa would have achieved greater success had he been born and educated in America. He had a photographic mind, being able to take a car engine apart and putting it back together so that it would work. He did the same with wristwatches. He enjoyed doing this as one enjoys doing puzzles. It was one of his favorite past times. We thought the world of grandpa and couldn't think of him being any different. He always bought us gifts on birthdays and special occasions, our first Holy Communion, confirmation, and graduation. When visiting his grandchildren, he would bring a shopping bag filled with cookies.

Grandpa was kind and loving. He would haul my brother, Lou, and I, around in a wagon for miles, until we were old enough to walk the far distances ourselves, which was from one nearby town to another. He didn't drive, so he walked and took buses. When being with him, he would tip his fedora and say hello to every lady he met, on the bus or wherever. I asked why he did this.

"I think I know her!" he replied.

It was his way of being a gentleman. One might say that he was flirting, but being in his forties and a widower, he had to answer to no one except the watchful eyes of his adult children. During grandpa's days, the 1930's, widows and widowers did not remarry as they do today. I think I took after grandpa, especially as I write this, being a widower myself. I should buy a fedora and be like him, tipping my hat and saying, "hello!" to every woman I run into. Who knows what might happen?

Grandpa was always a joy to be with. He kept his composure even after hard times, World War I, death of his wife, a grandchild (little Marie), and the loss of his properties during the great depression of 1929. The stock market crashed, people committed suicide, investors jumped out of tall buildings on Wall Street, having lost their fortunes, and then their lives. People lined up for blocks in the freezing cold in New York, hoping to get a job so they could buy food. They needed work and food. People were starving! Grandpa had to give up his two-story home, with a yard that had all kinds of fruit trees. For him, it was like giving up Italy once again. There were mulberries, gooseberries, figs, and a big cherry tree with branches hanging over the garage. My dad would get out the ladder, carry Lou and I up onto the garage so that we could lie on our backs and pick the cherries. The yard was big. We would play boccie ball, a wonderful Italian game

Grandpa had to give up all of this. He and his youngest son, Uncle Mike, then moved into an apartment having only one bed that they shared. His older children were on their own. It was now grandpa and Uncle Mike living in this musty room by themselves. Later, World War II erupted and things got worse before they got better. Uncle Charles, another son, joined the army and fought in the major battles of Europe. Dad, mom, Lou, and I moved into Mr. Katz's home, renting the second floor. It was here where my sister, Marion, was born. There were only two bedrooms, not enough room for Grandpa and Uncle Mike. This saddened my parents no end. It was the best they could do at the time, until my dad decided to take a bold step in 1942 (war still going on) and bought a home in a nearby town, called Flushing. Mom was worried about being able to afford this. She remembered that her father, grandpa, had lost his home and properties only several years before. The cost of the home was $5,000. They paid it off in five years, my dad working harder than ever, and mom being frugal with every penny she spent on food, shopping from store to store to save a penny. She had to walk and carry heavy grocery bags in her arms. My job was to put the coffee on the moment I saw her coming down the block. We never knew what the word "vacation" meant, or "dining out," but had the best mom, dad, and grandpa, in the whole world. What greater joy could there be than being with them?

The move from College Point to Flushing was like moving to another state, even though it was only ten miles away. I was now 12 years old, Lou 15 and baby Marion, 2. It meant going to another school, meeting new classmates, and neighbors on the street where our first and only owned home was during our childhood. It was a beautiful home, called a "bungalow," about 800 square feet, having two bedrooms, one bathroom, a parlor, small dining area, and a tiny kitchen. Before long, the basement was converted into several rooms, a large area for dining to have relatives over for food and drink. Another kitchen was built in the basement, making it easier for mom to prepare the big dinners, rather than having to run up and down to the kitchen upstairs.

All of my Uncles later got together once again to build a large room in the attic with "three single bunk beds" built into the walls. Why three, when there was only Lou and I to sleep upstairs? Our sister, Marion, was to have our room downstairs. My dad then dropped the bombshell telling mom why he did this.

"Tanella, I want your father to come and live with us!" he said.

Uncle Mike had married. Grandpa was living alone in this dingy room. Needless to mention, this brought tears to my mother's eyes, to think that her husband would be willing to give up much of his privacy for her father. Grandpa's other children may have wanted to do this, but for some reason weren't able to. Aunt Lena, my mother's younger sister, came to our home in tears, praising my dad for his sympathetic heart towards grandpa. It was also my parents who were generous to Aunt Lena, Uncle Carmen, and children, when they were going through hard times. One of their children, Marie, three years old had died. Mom and dad provided them with food and shoes in a manner that they didn't lose their dignity. More tears! More love!

Grandpa moved in with us and became our roommate. Bunk bed #1 was his! It meant more stories and laughter at night time when retiring, especially if we had beans for dinner. As always, we felt privileged to have grandpa live with us. He sat at the head of the table on one end and dad at the other. Mom and dad would have it no other way. Dad instructed mom that her father came first, before himself. Life in our new home took a turn for the better. Grandpa was no longer alone, my parents were happy to care for him. Lou, Marion, and I were overjoyed having him live with us, the only grandparent we ever knew. We really had to toe the line now, for grandpa was given full authority to reprimand us if necessary, which meant a triple whammy, first grandpa, then mom, and finally dad. We knew that they loved us, and we got only what we deserved. Grandpa played an important role in our lives, loving and caring for us as being very special.

After building the room in the basement and then in the attic, it was now time to build a garage. My Uncle Sylvester, my father's brother-in-law, was a contractor. He spearheaded the project and gave me an assignment (I was only 12). He plotted where the garage and foundation would go.

He then handed me a shovel and said, "Start digging!"

I thought he was joking, but after giving me the shovel, he said, "I'll be back in a week to see how far you got." Ha! Ha! I didn't get very far, so he brought in help, otherwise it would have taken years to complete the garage.

One following Sunday morning, about six a.m., Uncle Sylvester, other Uncles and bricklayers arrived. The bricks and bags of cement were delivered the day before. We had to mix the cement ourselves. So I got another assignment, in addition to carrying the bricks to the bricklayers. It was a wonderful experience to see this happening and to be a small part of it. The bricklayers knew their job when constructing the walls. Not one brick was out of alignment. All were even as could be. As noon approached and half of the bricks had been laid, it was time for lunch in the room built in the basement only months before. As expected, the spaghetti, meatballs, chicken, and salad were served in abundance. "Gallons of red wine" flowed endlessly. During lunch, Uncle Sylvester sang and played the accordion. Once lunch was over, it was back to work to finish the second half of the garage. The bricklayers apparently had too much wine to drink and were now feeling good. The bricks on the second half of the garage came out uneven. To this day we laugh about it, being able to see how perfect it was before lunch and how uneven afterwards. In spite of this, my dad was especially happy that he could now put his car in the garage.

"Make ah da Vino!" While living in Mr. Katz's home, every other year a truck loaded with grapes would pull up in front of the house. Dad, grandpa, and my Uncles would carry them down to the basement where the winepress was that grandpa had taken with him from the home he lost. I helped carry the grapes, another activity I enjoyed.. The winepress was in this basement where the furnace and coal bin were. Remember the dining room table that was cut up and placed in this furnace to keep us warm? Anyway, we dumped the grapes into the winepress and began crushing them. No! We didn't use our bare feet! The juice was then placed into barrels. The three barrels were kept in a separate room on a rack about two feet off the ground. The room was like a prison cell. Grandpa kept the key to the door; since he was in charge of "Make ah da Vino!"

As the weeks went by, grandpa would take a sip of the wine from each barrel to see how it was fermenting. Sometimes I think he took gulps rather than sips. We wondered, "When is grandpa coming back upstairs to let us know how the wine was coming along?" It turned out great! There was enough to last for a long time.

"More about grandpa" … He learned as a child, "don't drink the water in Italy," or anywhere else! Wine to him was like water is to us, except one too many would make him "tipsy." He didn't drive, so why worry? One Christmas day at Aunt Lena and Uncle Carmen's home, our families were together enjoying the celebration. As always, the wine flowed freely. During dinner, my sister, Marion, pointed out to grandpa that a string of lights weren't working on the Christmas tree. Grandpa got up from the table and wobbled "into" the Christmas tree, knocking it down. All hell broke loose! Everyone got excited to see if grandpa got hurt as he was lying under the tree. Once we knew that he was ok, we laughed our heads off. He himself laughed. What a Christmas gift! In addition to the manger and Holy Family under the tree, there also was grandpa for a few minutes. My cousin, Rose, recently called me from New York.

"Remember when grandpa knocked down the Christmas tree?" she asked.

That happened sixty years ago.

"In my heart lie these fond memories, like treasures of gold that one retrieves, of the good times and the bad, the joyful and the sad, I will always remember mom and dad. Grandpa too!"

Chapter 4
Living in Flushing

We now lived in our own home. The attic, basement, and garage, all complete. Behind our home were woods where pheasants and rabbits would nest and blackberry bushes which I enjoyed picking for mom so that she could make jam. Farther beyond, there were farms. There were pear trees along the streets. The ground was very fertile, great for planting vegetables behind our home. Grandpa took care of this and more. There had to be fig trees obviously. Grandpa nurtured them as a mother would her baby. When fall approached, he would wrap tar paper around the fig trees and bury them in the ground until Spring came. Grandpa had many secrets that he brought with him from Italy.

It was now time for Lou and me to find a job, since we could no longer go to dad's store to shine shoes. It was ten miles away. We couldn't leave at six in the morning with dad, although I would occasionally make it on a Saturday or in summertime. During a snowy winter season, I (12 years old) would shovel sidewalks for 50 cents. Had to do more than one to make a few dollars. It was cold out! My hands would freeze, but there was money to be made. One time Uncle Mike took me to College Point when a heavy snowfall tied up the town. The local city council hired us. They provided us with big shovels to clear the streets. While we got paid by the hour, Uncle Mike didn't want me out in the freezing cold (I was skinny and freezing). He took me to the nearest Catholic Church, St. Fidelis, and said, "You stay inside. I'll come back later to pick you up." What else was there to do, but pray that I would get paid?

When summer came, Lou and I would get work at the nearby farm picking tomatoes and string beans. It came to an abrupt end when I saw a snake in the cabbage patch. On we went looking for another type of job. We got work caddying at Bayside Golf Links which was beautiful, surrounded by farms. The pay was great. We never had it so good. We were out in the sunshine, getting nice and tan. After giving mom our earnings, she gave us a couple of dollars to enjoy. This meant more bow ties and colored socks. Perry Como, Babe Ruth, Ray Bolger, and other celebrities played at this golf course. It was exciting to see Perry Como once again after having attended his birthday party several years before. Did he remember me? No!

On Mondays, the golf course was closed, so we would go around the outside along the fence looking for lost golf balls that we could sell the next day. While looking for golf balls, I came across a box that had nice tiny cases inside, like the type that hold ten aspirins. While empty, I still took them home and put them in the drawer where mom would keep our underwear and pajamas. About a week later, mom got excited when she found the box and its contents.

"Who do these belong to?" she said nervously to Lou and me.

"Oh! Mom, they're mine," I said. "Aren't they cute?"

I don't know what I'll use them for?" she said. "Honey, mom's going to throw these away."

Being 12 years old, young and innocent, I didn't know what condoms were.

Each morning, before leaving to go caddying, mom would wake Lou and I up at 6:00 AM, so we could eat breakfast (oatmeal) and get to the golf course early which was a three mile walk. Getting there early meant we would have better chances of carrying more than one golf bag per golfer a day. While eating our oatmeal, mom would make these great sandwiches with fresh Italian bread loaded with salami, lettuce, tomatoes, and lots of mayonnaise. Was this the beginning of "Subways?" She would wrap the sandwich in wax paper; put it in a brown bag, which we would tuck around our belt. By the time we arrived at the golf course, I was already starving (oatmeal does that to me). I couldn't wait to eat my "sandwich," but had to until I finished the first loop (18 holes) that would be three hours later. While carrying the golf clubs for this customer and now approaching the 18th hole, my taste buds were going wild thinking I would soon be eating my sandwich. The customer made his last shot approaching the green. He walked ahead of me and a few feet from the green. "Quick! Give me a sandwich!" he yelled.

That's what it sounded like to me. So I dropped the golf bag, ran up to him, and handed him the "sandwich" mom made for me, thinking he needed food and would faint if he didn't have something to eat right away. He looked at me.

"No, no, no," he said. "I need the "sand wedge" (a golf club). I'm in the sand trap!"

Ha! Ha! How happy I was to think I could soon look forward to eating my "sandwich" (sand wedge?).

When not caddying, I would cut the front and back lawn at home. I did it meticulously, using grandpa's hatchet as an edger to keep the grass from growing over the sidewalk. I knew how happy it made dad when coming home from work to see the yard looking great. Grandpa wasn't too happy (dulled his hatchet). The neighbors also admired my work. Dad would give me two dollars for doing a good job. That was a lot of money, more bow ties and colored socks. When not caddying during the winter days, it was working at "P & C" vegetable market, delivering on a bicycle. Saturday night was payday, plus bags of fruit and vegetables to take home to mom and dad. I now felt like I was an adult (13 years old) bringing home money and food too.

We still had playtime, especially on Saturdays during the school year. I tried out for the basketball team, but after being constantly elbowed on the head, it wasn't for me. I then tried football, putting on the helmet, the knee and shoulder pads, and the cleats. Once I put all this on, I couldn't run for beans. The outfit weighed more than I did. Next was baseball that I enjoyed except for getting nervous when trying to catch a high fly ball. What sport was there for me to participate in? I truly loved sports, but I had to find the right one for a skinny little kid. Was it running that I was good at? Was running considered to be a sport?

While the wars were still going on, President Roosevelt died April 12th, 1945. Harry Truman became President. On April 28th,

Mussolini was hung by Italian partisans. Hitler committed suicide two days later. Three world leaders died one way or another within a three-week period. Strange, huh? The war in Europe ended May 8th, 1945, V-E Day (Victory in Europe). Truman wasted no time in bringing the war against Japan to an abrupt end by dropping the atomic bomb on Hiroshima, August 6th, 1945. Another on Nagasaki, August 9th. Japan surrendered on September 2nd, 1945, V-J Day (victory over Japan). We celebrated by someone driving their car slowly in the middle of the streets where we lived, while we marched along side beating on pots, pans, and carrying American flags. This was my first and last experience of drinking hard liquor with the adults.

In that same month, September, 1945, I started at Bayside High School which was a daily walk of about three-miles. It was across from the golf course where Lou and I caddied. One could not participate in sports during their freshman year. Besides, I couldn't play basketball, football, or baseball. The only sports left were swimming and track. I didn't like swimming. In my sophomore year, everyone had to run the class mile. It was a cold winter day. The track (pavement) was around a park, across from the school. Being in my bathing suit and very cold (it was winter), I hid behind a tree to block the wind, until it was time to run the mile. When the gun went off, I ran fast and hard, not to win, but to keep warm. Before I knew it, I was in the lead. Was this my cup of tea, to run, run, and run? On the last lap, I was out in front coming to the finish. My arms and legs were now tired. My chest was burning up. Other runners who hid behind trees until the last lap finished ahead of me. I crossed the finish line in five minutes and forty-five seconds, well enough for the track coach, Mr. George Wright, to ask me to join the track team. I didn't know that it was a competitive sport, competing against one another and other schools. I joined the team!

Now it meant reporting to Mr. Wright each day after classes to practice. The hard work began, running sprints for speed, and long distances for endurance. I would run until my head hurt. When arriving home, mom would see me limping from aching shin splints. This didn't go over well with her. She wanted me to quit running.

However, dad stepped in and said, "Tanella, he's going to run!"

Dad knew that this was the sport for me. He, Uncle Mike, and grandpa, then took over, encouraging me to go all the way, saying, "Do your best!" My track career was about to begin with their support. From then on, grandpa would say to me each day, "champeen of da woild!" Remember? He came from Italy and spoke broken English.

"It's love that really matters, and in our heart it sings, so dream my son, dream of wondrous things."

Chapter 5
Our Faith

We were brought up as Catholic, to believe in God and Jesus. I went to parochial grammar school, then to public high school. When entering Bayside High, my faith meant more to me than anything, never to be changed. It played an important role in my life and running career.

Lou, Marion, and I had to go to Confession and Holy Communion at least twice a month. On those Sundays, when going to mass, mom would not make meatballs and spaghetti for Sunday dinner (2:00 pm) knowing that we were fasting from midnight until receiving Holy Communion. She didn't want us to wake up that morning to the smell of meatballs cooking. It would have been torture for us not to have one, or two, before going to mass. We, therefore, went to an early mass on those days, around nine o'clock. After mass, we would stop by the German bakery to buy Kaiser rolls and buns. Once we got home, around 10 o'clock, mom would give us a cup of coffee, half coffee and half milk, with lots of sugar, so that when we dunked the buttered Kaiser rolls and buns, it would taste great! This made fasting and going to Communion worth it (our reward).

On those Sundays, mom would make a "leg of lamb, with small baked potatoes, and rice." She would then pour the gravy, made from the juice of the roast, over the lamb, rice and potatoes. I have never tasted anything as good as this, except when she made the roast beef (medium pink), mashed potatoes, and red cabbage. Oh! This is killing me! I would pay $100.00 just to have a little taste of these dinners. Mom could make anything taste good. How lucky we were to have mom, dad, and grandpa.

Life did change in Flushing for the better. Dad worked as hard as he could, grandpa got a job as a night watchman, and mom took care of the home. We felt rich, having milk, bread, and meat delivered to our home. In the wintertime, when the milk was delivered, it was placed in a container by the door, outside. The cream from the milk, because of the freezing weather, would pop to the top of the bottle, about an inch high. The Italian bread was fresh and crispy, great with butter for dunking in coffee. Grandpa always took hard bread from the breadbox and dunked it in coffee, no butter or sugar. This was his breakfast all of his life. Dare to make him bacon and eggs would cause him to become upset.

The meat was delivered exactly the way mom wanted it, otherwise it was sent back. Before deciding to have it delivered, mom made several trips by bus to the butcher shop that was about ten-miles away. Once the butcher knew exactly what mom wanted, she had him deliver it in the future which saved her time and bus fare (5 cents). A truck also pulled up in front of our home with Italian groceries, canned tomatoes, and pasta. A little ladder, a few steps high, enabled mom to go inside the enclosed truck to decide what she wanted. Lots of peddlers did this (the Greco family) to make a living. Why wait for someone to come to your store (if you were lucky to have one) when you could bring it to their home?

For other groceries, the eggs and vegetables, mom would walk from one store to another, looking and bargaining for specials. She wouldn't just accept the advertised special price. I know this for a fact, since I would be with her

"Mom, c'mon! Let's go home. I'm tired!" I'd say. This is how she saved all that money for dad to make his trip to Italy. I always said that mom could have run IBM and made them greater profits. Mom and grandpa were a home team to be reckoned with, grandpa taking care of the yard and plumbing, while mom did the painting, in addition to her other chores. Dad had no spare time for this. I think he was happy that he didn't,

My parents taught us that God was #1 in our lives, the family next. We had a bible and a few statues in our home. For whatever reason, I began reading the bible diligently during my first year at

Bayside High School. I later decided to offer up my track races to God, for His greater honor and glory. He didn't need me, but I needed Him. How could I go wrong being on His team? Before each race, I would make the sign of the cross, offering it up to God, asking Him to give me the "strength" to do my best, sometimes to win. Nothing gave me greater pleasure than making the sign of the cross at the start of the 5,000 meter run at the 1952 Olympic Games in Helsinki, Finland, knowing there were thousands of communists watching and a few participating in my race. This meant as much to me as placing in the finals (which I didn't).

"Keep trying son, do your best, win or lose, its love that really matters!"

* * *

THE FRAGRANCE AND JOY OF EASTER

Easter! What wonderful memories. Why would I now recall at my age, 76, the joy of Easter? It was exactly that, not only because of the celebration of the risen Christ, but also of the things my parents did on that day so we would never forget it and be forever thankful.

As Easter week approached, my Dad, a cobbler, would take time out from work to take us out to get an entire outfit, new shoes, a suit, shirt, and tie. He was a proud man of the manner in which he dressed and wanted his children to likewise look their best, especially on Easter. Mom trusted Dad with this duty knowing that he himself was immaculate the way he dressed, having his suits and ours made to order.

While Dad was busy with us, Mom was preparing for Easter day's feast. She would bake everything imaginable! For the dinner on that day, which began around 2 P.M., after attending Mass and going to the "hot-house" with Dad to buy flowers for Mom, she would have the table set with her finest linens, china, and silverware. The cakes and cookies were placed on display, near the dining room table, out of reach from us children, to be enjoyed after we ate our dinner. We always had room for these goodies, even though we stuffed ourselves on the main course, soup, roasts, chicken, potatoes, and vegetables. Of course, there had to be pasta, meatballs, braciole, and salad with olive oil and wine vinegar. Lots of food? You bet! Even though my mother made turkey or roasts, with all the trimmings, Dad had to have his pasta and meatballs. Hey! That's Italian.

Mom, being the oldest of six children, caring for them and her father at the young age of sixteen when her mother passed away, was greatly respected and loved by them. When they became adults and married, they would either have dinner with us on that day, or stop by later for coffee and dessert. When they did, they brought us children the thickest and most wonderful chocolate bunnies that lasted us for two weeks. Great during the movies. Wow! Hard boiled colored eggs, jelly beans, and chocolate bunnies.

Is it any wonder why I remember Easter at my age? In addition, the important events leading up to this was the week of mourning Christ's passion and suffering. It was truly all about Him! My parents made sure that we went to Church on Good Friday from 12 o'clock until 3. It was the longest three hours of my life. Prayers and stations of the cross. At the end of the three hours, it was kissing Jesus's feet on the cross which to us children appeared life size. We couldn't eat meat on that day until noon the following day, nor play the radio. No tv existed then.

On Easter day, I loved the beautiful fragrance in the air outside our home, blossoms and flowers, enjoying it as much as I enjoyed the wonderful aroma inside, Mom's baking, the roasts cooking, and the smell of the meatballs and pasta.

Christmas was very much the same, another celebration and feast. On Christmas eve, Mom would tuck us in bed about 8 0' clock, saying that Santa was on his way and she and Dad would wake us after he arrived. Being sound asleep, my parents would later awaken us, saying that Santa just left to visit other children. What a great feeling to look under the glistening Christmas tree and all the presents.

Thank you, Mom and Dad. Thank you, God. Thank you, Santa Claus, for making our childhood so wonderful.

Chapter 6
"Bayside High School Days"

Now a sophomore, it was wonderful to be able to run each day with the track team. I still didn't know what distance was truly best for me. I tried the sprint races, but didn't have that burst of speed required for the 100 and 220 yard dash. Then the 440, still not good enough to impress Mr. Wright. He knew all the time what the right distance was for me, but never discouraged me from finding out for myself. It was the mile run!

After practicing with the team milers, I began to improve. Practice and hard work paid off. About a month later, I cut my mile time down by thirty seconds, running five minutes and fifteen seconds. This made me realize what one can do by practicing and working hard. I continued to do so not knowing that Mr. Wright would eventually have me run against the top miler, John Meehan, whom I admired and wanted to be like. John pulled me along to a personal best under five minutes. He won, but it wasn't long before I could stay up with him. He was a great source of encouragement.

Before I knew it, Mr. Wright entered me in some races. I came in third or fourth, but knew for sure that I wanted to be a great miler. Bayside's school record was 4 minutes and 26 seconds set by Alan Hillman who was killed in the war. It seemed impossible to beat that time. As far as I was concerned, Alan was immortal. I loved him even though I never met him. Mr. Wright continued to train me and build my confidence, along with my dad, Uncle Mike, and grandpa. Mom still didn't like the idea of me running.

Training included long distance running to build endurance

and stamina. We had to run around the outside of the golf course where Lou and I use to caddy and look for golf balls. Memories came to mind about the box and cases that mom found in my drawer by my underwear and pajamas. This and the sandwich (sand wedge) episode became lasting jokes in my lifetime, not to mention "the rolling meatballs!" Running around the golf course was about two-miles. It was perfect training for cross-country races that I would later participate in. The longer the race, the better I was. It was the mile run during my sophomore year. The following year it was both, cross-country and the mile run.

At the beginning of my junior year, the war had been over for two years. During dinner mom looked at dad and said, "Joe, Why are you so sad?"

"Tanella, I would like to go to Italy to see the family I left behind when I was seventeen. I would also like to go to my parent's grave," he said.

"Joe, go!" Mom said.

"How can I, Tanella? We don't have that kind of money."

Mom got up from the table, went into their bedroom, and came back with a wad a dough, handed it to him,

"This should be enough for you to go."

My father couldn't believe it, nor could we, Lou, Marion, and I.,

"Tanella, where did you get all of this money?" Dad asked.

Mom explained that when he gave her money to run the household, she would do everything to save a penny here and there by looking for the best prices when shopping for food and necessities. She never bought anything for herself. There was almost enough money for her to go too, but she couldn't leave Marion behind, who was only five years old. Grandpa then got up from the table, went to his bedroom, bunk bed#1, and came back with enough money for all three of them to go, dad, mom, and Marion. Off they went! Lou and I searched under our mattresses wondering if we too would come up with money. Zero! While they were gone, Aunt Lena watched over us. Lou and I watched over grandpa, especially when he would tip his fedora to the ladies.

While my parents and Marion were in Italy, I established

myself as a runner to be contended with, having won the 2 mile Queens Borough Cross Country Championship. We were so happy when my parents returned, having been gone for four weeks. They traveled by ship and thought they would never survive the treacherous ocean. My sister, only five years old, began talking in Italian to my brother and me. That must be the age to learn a language. It was so cute to hear her say, "Parlare Italiano, Luigi?"

Lou and I couldn't respond and wondered what happened to her. Now was the time to break the good news to them. Dad got so excited when handed the newspaper article.

"George Capozzoli wins!" Don't know why "George?" Instead of "Charlie," but it was me.

Mom now began to have second thoughts about my running. She joined dad, Uncle Mike, and grandpa in encouraging me to do my best. My other uncles, aunts, and cousins also became fans and cheered me on. Grandpa's voice echoed through out our Home, "Champeen of da Woild!"

"Dream my son, dream of wondrous things, its love that really matters"

George Cappozolli Aims For City Championship Following Crown Here

Newtown Harriers Win Title As Bayside Takes 2nd Place

Bayside High School may not win the City cross-country championship on Saturday at Van Cortlandt Park, but one of its representatives may gain individual honors. George Cappozolli the Commodore's ace harrier, gave strong indication of copping the individual crown by winning the Queens championship late last Tuesday.

Cappozolli ran a fine race in winning his title in the time of 13:45. A strong sprint near the finish line enabled "Cappy" to beat Tom Coulter of Newtown by ten yards.

Newtown Wins Title

Newtown won team honors with the Baysiders grabbing the runner-up spot. In winning, Newtown placed five men in the first ten. The Commodores picked up two positions in the first ten; Cappozolli and George Reidleheuber who finished sixth.

For Bayside, Don Fredericks, Dick Frey, Joe Prescott and Fred Kirchoff placed in the top section of the finishers. Frey might have

Cappozolli, of Bayside, Victor in P.S.A.L. Run

Charles Capozzoli, of Bayside, one of the top scholastic distance runners in the city, turned in the best individual performance in the second P. S. A. L. weekly cross-country run at Van Cortlandt Park yesterday. Capozzoli, leading all the way, covered the two and a quarter mile course in 13:54.5, finishing twenty-five yards ahead of George Helfenstein, of Ft. Hamilton, in Group 3. Randy Philpotts, of Morris, won the Group 1 run in 13:58.4 and Al Fosker, who upset Robert Audolensky, of Bronx Science, City P. S. A. L. Harrier Champion, scored his second victory in a row, taking Group 2 honors in 14:19.

Bayside High turned in the low score of the fifty-five competing schools by taking the Group 3 run with forty points. Andrew Jackson won the team title for the second successive week in Group 1 with seventy-seven points and Brooklyn Automotive took the honors in Group 2 with seventy six points.

Chapter 7
"Hard Work, Aches,
Pains, and Angels?"

Now that mom accepted the fact that running track was the sport for me, I trained harder than ever. It was practice every day of the week, sometimes on Sunday. The aches and pains became worse. I thought, maybe mom was right from the very beginning?

Shin splints were torture. There were no remedies. Bayside High had no whirlpool baths or trainer to rub and massage ones aching muscles. My parents decided to buy me an infrared ray heat lamp believing it would help. I applied as much heat as I could bear. Then, rubbed and massaged my legs with salve, wrapping towels around them. Oh! This felt so good and worked after many applications. During the treatments, I read sports magazines about the flying parson, Gil Dodds, a sub 4:10 miler, Glenn Cunningham, America's greatest, and Gunder Hagg who held the world record for the mile, 4:02. Practice went on as usual. Trainers today would most likely say that applying heat to shin splints was dangerous, but it worked for me!

I began to run in dual meets and various championship events, coming in third, or fourth. This was in my junior year. Finally, I won a race in New Jersey in the slow time of 4:42, but good enough to win a beautiful trophy. Mr. Wright, my coach, dropped me off in front of my home where mom was waiting on the front porch.

When she saw me, she said, "What's that in your arms?"

I tried to cover it up and yelled, "Mom, I won! This beautiful trophy is mine forever!"

Mom placed the trophy on the fireplace mantel, where dad would immediately see it when arriving home. Dad entered the front door, saw the trophy, and tears began rolling down his face. He knew what happened, and said, "Charlie, come with me. I'm going to buy a bottle of whiskey to celebrate!"

In my mind I thought, oh, no! Remembering my experience when celebrating the end of the wars in 1945."

It was a long time from then on before I won another race, coming in third or fourth.

One night my dad said, "How did you do today?" As I was going to answer, he interrupted me. "You always have an excuse."

My heart sank. Was this my #1 fan giving up on me? He asked no more questions. I went to my room very depressed. The following week, I cut down on my training, took several days off, and didn't care that I was going to run in Madison Square Garden the coming

Saturday. I even questioned God's goodness, the one whom I offered up my races to, for His greater honor and glory. When Saturday arrived, instead of having a poached egg on toast and a cup of tea for breakfast, I asked mom to make me a salami sandwich to take with me to the Garden. Mom knew my heart and didn't question me.

As soon as I got to Madison Square Garden in early afternoon, I went to the concession stand and bought a cup of coffee to go with the sandwich. I devoured it! It tasted better than the usual poached egg and tea. Besides I didn't care anymore. For awhile I became a spectator watching some of the races that were going on. Now it was time to warm up and report to the start of the mile run, as announced over the PA system. I didn't wear my usual white socks. Instead I wore ugly black socks (my dad's?) And looked like someone who came off the street.

I took my position at the start and said to myself, "This is your last race!"

The gun went off! I sprinted as fast as I could to take the lead. Usually I stayed in the pack, getting shoved around and elbowed. I'm now in the lead waiting for the star milers to pass me. It wasn't happening. I felt extremely good. With four laps to go (its eleven laps to the mile indoors), I felt like Angels were carrying me around the track. I began lapping other runners, crossing the finish line in my best time ever, 4:26, setting a meet record. It electrified the crowd, college and high school coaches included. Of course, I couldn't wait to get home. My dad didn't ask me how I did. Mom already knew. The next day dad was reading the sports pages in the Sunday New York Times. The headlines across the top of the page from one end to the other, "Capozzoli Shatters Meet Record in Annexing School Mile!"

My dad was too shocked and too happy to say anything. We sat down at the dinner table, we're thankful to God for my victory, and our beautiful family. From then on, I won all the remaining mile runs in my senior year. Throughout our home you could hear grandpa's voice echoing, "Champeen of da Woild!"

SPORTS   THE NEW YORK TIMES, SUNDAY, FEBRUARY 27, 1949.

Capozzoli Shatters Meet Record

BAYSIDE ACE VICTOR IN 4:26.3 AT GARDEN

Capozzoli Clips Old Record by Four Seconds to Defeat Mulligan of Loughlin

---

DOWDEN TAKES HALF-MILE

Carton of Iona Runs Second —Branch of Boys Is Upset as Lohr Wins Sprint

Charles Capozzoli of Bayside High School set a meet record of 4:26.3 in the one-mile run, to provide the feature of the interscholastic track program at Madison Square Garden yesterday afternoon, in conjunction with the trials of the Intercollegiate A. A. A. championships.

Running the race of his life, the 18-year-old Queens youngster shaved four full seconds off the mark set two years ago by William Lucas of Morris, now a Manhattan freshman. Capozzoli, who never before had broken 4:30, led his nearest opponent by nearly eighty yards.

He took the lead with six laps to go and pulled steadily away from the field. Heading the out distanced pursuit was Alan Mulligan of Bishop Loughlin. Third place went to Randy Philpotts of Morris, runner-up last Saturday in the National A. A. U. interscholastic mile championship, in which Capozzoli finished fourth.

Wins by Five Yards

Bishop Loughlin's Marrott Dowden, narrowly beaten for the National AAU interscholastic 1,000-yard crown last week, took the half-mile in convincing style. The Brooklyn runner won by five yards, trailing him in order were Patrick Carton of Iona, Edward Brandstoettner of Xavier and Roy Lucas of Loughlin.

These races, open to both the Public Schools Athletic League and the Catholic High Schools Athletic Association, were run in sections, but in each case the medal winners came from the same section.

Eagle Sports Picture

CAUSES BIG SURPRISE—Charles Capozzoli, right, Bayside, winning the combined P. S. A. L.-C. H. S. A. A. mile run in the interscholastic part of the I.C.4-A track and field championships yesterday at Madison Square Garden in record time of 4:26.3. The runner on the left is being lapped. Al Mulligan, Loughlin, was second and Randy Philpotts, Morris, the choice, was third.

By now, I thought I had it made. No one could beat me. Guess what happens? I'm scheduled to run against Fred Dwyer of Seton Hall Prep, the top miler in New Jersey. The event is to take place in Englewood, New Jersey, the same track where I won the year before in 4:42, taking first place and receiving my first trophy. I never met Dwyer before. Had no idea how fast he could run. The track was soggy that day from early morning rain. The gun went off. I took the lead, figuring I would psyche him out. I was running in the third lane. The first and second lanes had puddles and were too soggy to run in. I held the lead for the first three laps, not knowing exactly where Dwyer was, until the gun went off for the final lap. I then knew exactly where he was. He whizzed by me, running in the second lane with a burst of speed, gaining a good ten-yard lead. With 220 yards to go, he increased his lead to 20 yards. I was now about to give up when I said to myself, "Do your best. He could be on his way to breaking the National High School record. Nothing wrong with being second."

With Dwyer burning up the track, I'm now talking to myself, "What do you tell dad? No excuses! You haven't lost a race since running that 4:26 mile." Suddenly those Angels came into play. I came down the straight-a-way 15 yards behind Dwyer with only 100 yards to go to the finish. I began sprinting like never before, rapidly gaining on him. We both crossed the finish line at the same time, 4:22.9, only one and seven tenths off the National High School record (picture on cover). My chest had broken the tape as Dwyer was beginning to collapse.

This reminded me of my dad's comment many years ago when he said, "You had the chest of an athlete when you were born."

My coach, Mr. Wright, was in the center of the track during the race, but seeing me 20 yards behind with 220 yards to go, he turned his head and didn't watch the finish. I immediately ran up to him after crossing the finish line.

"You've had a great year. You can't win them all," he said.

"Mr. Wright, I won! I won!" I said and knelt down and prayed until it was announced over the PA system.

"Capozzoli, winner of the one mile run in 4:22.9, a new meet record."

Dwyer and I became the best of friends from then on, later running in Europe against the finest runners in the world. Dwyer concentrated on the mile and I on the longer distances. Dwyer became one of the greatest milers in the world, close to breaking the four minute mile.

"Never give up, do your best, win or lose, its love that really matters. Believe in God and His Angels!"

Run To Win
Love And Sacrifice

Tributes Better Than Trophies to Her

Capozzoli, Unspoiled by Track Fame, Recalls First Victory Was Winning Mother as Fan

Schenectady Mark Broken By Capozzoli

By Rod Thomas

Tanella Capozzoli was praying. The next day her son, Charley, would try for the United States Olympic team. The mother of Georgetown University's crack distance runner asked only that nothing prevent him from turning in his best performance, that injury or illness would not deprive him of a chance to go to Helsinki.

In Los Angeles for the Olympic trials, Charley was not at all assured of success, even if in perfect fettle for the 5,000-meter test. He wasn't the runner he is today, a year later—at the moment preparing for his last race as a collegian.

On that evening a year ago in the modest Capozzoli home in College Point, Queensboro, N. Y., his mother's thoughts of Charley were tinged with self-reproach—for having attempted to cut short his athletic career. When Charley came limping home from high school, what with blisters, shin splints and charleyhorses, Mrs. Capozzoli rebelled against athletics. But not Papa Capozzoli. Charley continued to run.

Finally Won Trophy.

He didn't do so well. There were many seconds, thirds and fourths. Then, in a meet at Inglewood, N. J., Charley won an important race—and a big trophy.

Approaching home he hid the trophy under his jersey. His mother was quick to note the bulge—

"Charley, what is it?"

The boy grinned, whipped out the large, glistening object before his mother's startled eyes. "Where—where—did you get that?" she gasped.

"I won it," the boy said.

The light in his mother's eyes matched the sparkle of the trophy. Charley had another track fan.

Well Liked in College.

There were to be many other trophies, but more important to Mrs. Capozzoli, warm tributes to her son. At Georgetown he was to become as much esteemed for

CHARLEY CAPOZZOLI.

personal qualities as for athletic accomplishments.

It was to be said of him by Brutus Hamilton, head coach of the 1952 Olympic track team: "I think if I were to mention anyone as typical of the fine spirit of this team it would be Charley Capozzoli. He ran far and away the best race of his life—even though he didn't score."

He was to run the fastest two miles ever credited to an American still in college (8:55.5 in the Boston K. of C. meet); the fastest three miles ever run by an American (13:51.8 in a post-Olympic meet in England); smash the IC-4A two-mile record with a 9:00.2 performance; set an IC-4A five-mile cross-country record of 24:30.1; set an NCAA four-mile cross-country record of 10:36.7, and hang up sundry other marks in dual meets.

In a chat with Capozzoli at Georgetown yesterday, we wanted to know: "What victory gave you the most satisfaction?" Which brings us back to the opening paragraph.

Prayer Answered Quickly.

"It wasn't exactly a victory," Charley said. "It was the quick answer to a prayer. My mother thought I was to run in Los An-geles on a Saturday. I ran Friday.

"I finished third and made the team.

"Then I phoned home. Mother answered the phone. She said that when it rang she was praying things would go well with me 'tomorrow.' Then I told her, 'Mother, I made the team TODAY!'

"She said, 'You'—

"Then there was silence, for quite some time. I was afraid she'd fainted. I shouted, 'Mother, are you all right?'"

Charley grinned. "She was okay. Just speechless."

Then Charley Capozzoli summed up his philosophy of foot racing, and it was tantamount to what seems to be the life philosophy of this son of a shoemaker who won the heart of a university.

"I enjoy running for its sake alone, but not to win, just to be winning. I know when I do win, it will help to make somebody else happy. For this I am grateful to Providence."

This Saturday in Lincoln, Nebr., Charley Capozzoli, an all-time star at a university which has known many great trackmen, will finish his collegiate career in the 2-mile event of the NCAA championships. A graduate of the Foreign Service School, he may return to Georgetown to study law. The Hoyas hope he will, just to have him around.

Bayside Star Runs Mile in 4:25.5; Schertzer Wins Hurdles

(Special to the Sunday Press)

SCHENECTADY, N. Y., May 25—Charlie Capozzoli, Bayside High track star, reeled off an impressive 4:25.5 to capture the mile run in record time today in the ninth annual Schenectady Interscholastic Sports Carnival.

The Queens ace lowered the old meet standard, set by Rudolph Sims of DeWitt Clinton in 1942, by three and one-half seconds. Capozzoli's brilliant performance highlighted the 15-event track and field program, which saw 30 high schools participating and two other records established.

Bill Schertzer, a teammate of Capozzoli, was the victor in the 120-yard high hurdlers. His time was 15.9 seconds.

Andrew Jackson High won the 2½ mile medley relay Jack Thomas (880) John Sheldon (440) Jim Nugent (½ mile) and Ed Poweles (mile) establishing a mark of 11:17.4. This event was run for the first time replacing the one and ½ mile medley relay. East New York was second.

Boys High of Brooklyn monopolized the meet by winning four events and tying for first in an-

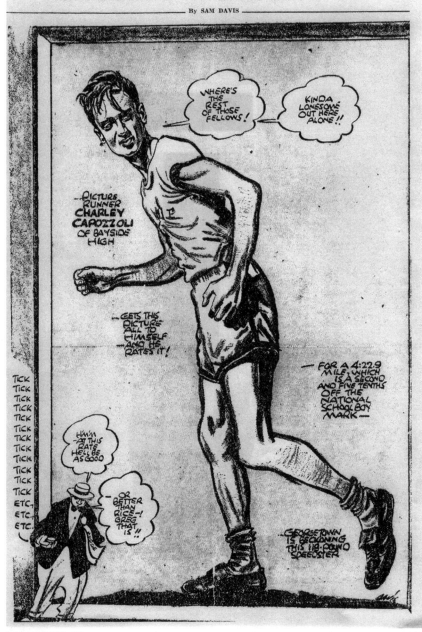

FacultyFacts

By Julia Willis

Bayside's one and only track coach, Mr. George Wright, has contributed modestly but unceasingly his time, efforts, and talent, to help put Bayside's track team into the limelight.

Mr. Wright came to Bayside in 1937 and the following year tackled the job of coaching the cross country team which would some day fulfill his ambition by becoming bigger and better. In 1944, he assumed the duties as a track coach. He has already gone down in sports history as helping to develop such notables as the late Alan Hillman, Lee Weber, Lenny Grace and Charlie Capozzoli.

Strange as it may seem, track has been Mr. Wright's life interest as he was a member of Cornell's team. He also entered the Queen's relay races, coached both Massachusetts' Berkshire School and Richmond Hill High School track teams before coming to Bayside and in his spare time now trains his 6 year old son to become a champion.

The Science of Biology is more conducive to Mr. Wright's intellectual interests as he may often be found doing extensive research in the field besides teaching it as a profession. Even though his classes learn the required work plus additional interesting facts, thanks to his extensive knowledge, they inevitably have a sample of his good humor. Not so long ago, while conducting his class one afternoon, he calmly remarked that there had been two snakes in that empty container—this started a snake-hunt under the radiators, in corners and behind desks.

CAPPY-ON RUNNING
'You're Made for the Track'

By ED GREFE   John Carroll

Charley Capozzoli, who runs the two-mile event in today's NCAA track meet, credits his high school coach for giving him his start in track.

"My gym teachers, George Wright and Lou Werner told me that either you're made for track or it was made for you."

"It was they who started me in track and still give me courage today telling me of all the set records that I can and should break." said Cappy.

When he was 15 he started at Bayside High in Flushing, N. Y. and was looking yearningly at that long mile when he was encouraged to try running it. Of course then he did not do it in the 4:07.8 that he is capable of doing now.

Then, too, he did not think that someday he would have a four year scholarship at Georgetown University, be breaking almost all records, and wearing the U. S. uniform in the '52 olympics, where he placed 7th ahead of the other U. S. runners.

"Any runner should have confidence in himself and in God and a lot of perseverance. He should also stay away from smoking, drinking, or any other thing that would be damaging to his career. A distance runner should not paticipate in any other sport as the mile and two mile demand all of one's attention if they want to keep in shape. Everyone should participate in some sport as it will keep them in physical shape and keep there mind on something wholesome," were words to the wise passed on by Cappy, who recently said something to the effect when he attended Roosevelt high to address the students.

High school trackmen who wish to attend college should remember that good grades are necessary to stay on the team but Capozzoli stated that his high school grades were not too hot, but he has kept a B average all thru his four years at the University and he has found out that with his grades high he can keep his mind on the meet and not be worried about the big exam coming up. So, then a good student is a better competitor.

Bayside High Track Team

Georgetown University

Georgetown University

Chapter 8
"So Long Bayside,
Hello Georgetown."

It was graduation night at Bayside, June 1949. I was given a great applause for my achievements, especially when it was announced that I received a scholarship to Georgetown University. Why I selected Georgetown, after receiving offers and visiting other universities, I really don't know? Never did see the Georgetown campus or meet the young newly hired coach, Frank Sevigne. After the graduation ceremonies, there was a celebration at home with my family, aunts, uncles, and cousins (my fan club). Mom baked my favorite double-decker cake topped with whip cream and canned slice peaches. Oh! How good it was!

The memories of graduation night and the friendships made will always be treasured. My teammates went different ways. John Golde, Larry Cody, and Bill Schertzer accepted scholarships to other universities. John was Bayside's great half miler, Larry, an outstanding miler, and Bill, the top hurdler. It was Shertzer's home where we would go Saturday nights after competition to party, sandwiches, soda, cookies, and girls! To this day, John and Larry still get together. Bill has since passed away. Goldie is one of my dearest of friends. I hope to attend his 50th wedding anniversary in May. His wife, Jeane, is his childhood sweetheart, as lovely as can be. Her twin sister, Kay, was recently visiting her son in California. We got together for lunch, reminisced about our high school days, and the fun times together. Our good friend, Bert Davison, continues to correspond.

A kind word can go a long way. Several of us Bayside students met in front of a movie theater in Flushing, the RKO. As we were talking, a black man passed behind me. He was limping and hunchback. I heard him say to himself, "I'm no good. No one cares for me!"

I turned my head and whispered to him, "You're ok. God loves you."

He stopped, turned around, and came toward us, asking, "Who said that?"

Fear set in not knowing if he was upset. I said, "I did," and then worried what he was going to do.

He took my hand, kissed it, and went on his way. This taught me of the importance of being kind to one another. We all need love! Our family members frequently say to one another, "I love you. God bless!" We also say this to our dear friends. It's a wonderful thing to say to your spouse and children, "I love you!" Try it. You will be amazed at the results. Some people go through life never hearing these wonderful words, "I love you. God bless!"

Summertime went by real fast. It was now time, September 1949, to leave for Georgetown to begin my freshman year. Was I crazy leaving mom, dad, grandpa, Lou, and Marion? There were also aunts, uncles and cousins whom I would greatly miss. I then remembered, dad left Italy and his family at the age of seventeen to come to America. My going to college, the first in our family, was to make my parents proud. Besides, I would return after completing college. Little did I know that I would return only during the holidays and summer vacations. Bunk bed #3 would become available after I graduated from Georgetown. It became Uncle Charles' when he retired from the Army. He lived there the remainder of his life. How kind and loving it was of my parents to first accept grandpa, then Uncle Charles, to live with them. Had I returned home to live, Lou would have had to share bunk bed #2, a twin bed, with me. Ha! Ha!

My parents drove me to Georgetown in Washington D.C. We toured the campus. It was quaint and beautiful. I registered and was assigned to my room.

Mom and dad then said, "good luck, son, we love you!"

There was a hug and a kiss and a tearful goodbye. I wanted to go home with them. They were my life. They were more important to me than anything in the world. How could I ever leave them, even for one day? I would miss mom's cooking and the great family dinners. What about Lou, Marion, Uncle Mike, and grandpa, "champeen of da woild!" After my parents left, being very depressed, I settled down in my room, which was near the campus bell tower that would ring out every hour on the hour, or was it every 15 minutes? My roommate was a great sprinter from Canada, Don Stonehouse. With his Canadian lingo and my New York accent, we had one heck of a time understanding each other. What did you say?

Freshman year in the school of Foreign Service required long hours of study. Two thirds of the class flunked out by the end of the first semester. I wasn't the most intelligent or industrious student when it came to reading Aristotle's Politics or Plato's Republic. I ended up in Dr. Quigley's class, a brilliant lay professor, whom everyone feared. Of all things, I passed his course, but flunked English for failing to interpret a poem on the final exam. I challenged the professor as to why. He said it meant something entirely different than what came to my mind. How could it mean something different than what it meant to me? I repeated the course.

While we had to practice track daily during our freshman year, we couldn't compete, except in one or two events for freshman and against other teammates. This wasn't easy to accept, first leaving home and now not being able to run in track competition. This convinced me that I must be crazy. It was depressing! To add to this, my heart broke when one of Georgetown's sensational sprinters, James Fielding became ill and died in his freshman year. This again was one of the saddest things I ever experienced, reminding me of when my three year old cousin, Marie, died. It left me with serious doubts about life in general. Later mom and I discussed how one goes on in life knowing that you can be gone from this earth in a moment, "without notice?" I was thinking of mom and dad.

Mom comforted me by saying, "don't worry about it, son. Go on with life as you are now doing."

I also found great consolation in daily visits to Dahlgren Chapel to pray and talk to Jesus. He became more real now than ever. Many of us students visited the Chapel frequently, especially before exams and races. I was forever grateful to my parents for the faith they taught me in my youth. Dahlgren Chapel was and still is centered in the middle of other buildings. One couldn't pass by it without stopping in. Most students went to confession, mass, and communion at least twice during the week.

Mr. Wright, my high school coach, sent me a detailed letter in my freshman year stating that I should immediately begin training very hard for the 1952 Olympics, the Olympics being three years away. While I was elated to think he thought so much of me, I said to myself, "maybe he's gone crazy too!" However, I listened to his advice. He was a great mentor and inspiration to me in high school. The long hours of training began with the dream that I would someday be a member of the 1952 Olympic Team, the games to be held in Helsinki, Finland. A teammate saw how hard I began training and said to me, "Charlie, if you continue to train as hard as you do, you're going to end up in Georgetown's hospital," which was adjacent to the track where we practiced. I believed in Mr. Wright and myself. Eventually I made the "52 Olympic Team," along with Mae Faggs, another Bayside product of Mr. Wright. Several years later, two more Bayside trackmen made Olympic teams in the walking events. Mr. George Wright was a great man and coach.

Letters kept coming from mom and dad encouraging me on. They sent me $5.00 dollars a week for postage stamps and an occasional phone call. No! I didn't buy bow ties or flashy colored socks. On campus, we had to wear shirts, ties, and jackets. This was Georgetown's dress code which reminded me of dad's in his shoe repair shop. The freshman school year came to an end and back home I went for the last summer vacation that I would spend there. I got a job in a factory for the summer, continued practicing (remembering Mr. Wright's advice), and gave my earnings to mom, not knowing that she was saving it for me, which came in handy later.

Sophomore year at Georgetown then began. It was easier to accept, knowing that I would run in track competition. In the State of Washington, I ran second in the NCAA's to Don Mc Ewen of Canada, running a 9:04 two-mile, the fastest ever run by a sophomore. This convinced my college coach that I was a better two miler than a miler. Therefore, he had me concentrate on the longer distance races.

I began to feel happier in my sophomore year making close friends with other students and teammates, Joe Deady, 1,000 yard and half-mile star, Dave Boland, half-mile great, Ed Kirk, mile champ. We have maintained our friendship to this day, along with Vince Kelly, 440 Ace, Pete Fedak, star hurdler, our team manager, Chuck Boyle, and my roommate and dear friend, Al Triandafilou.

Another summer vacation came, that wonderful time to go home. While having lunch with the family, there was a phone call for me. When returning to the table, my parents asked what it was all about.

Excited I said, "It was Mr. Ferris of the AAU asking if I would go to Europe during the summer with four other selected athletes to represent America in track competition."

Before I knew it, my bags were packed. Mom accompanied me to meet the other athletes. She asked if they would please watch over me, being twenty and the youngest in the group.

Our first stop was Reykjavik, Iceland. I competed in the 1,500 and 3,000 meter run, winning and setting records in both. When not competing or practicing, I played kickball with the children, only to find out later that I was being closely watched by the communists. Why? I wasn't any good in playing kickball (soccer). After two weeks in Iceland, we flew to Norway where a fresh Norwegian team awaited our arrival. Oslo was beautiful. The people were very friendly. I was to run the mile against the Norwegian champion, Karl Vefling. It was expected that he would make me look like a novice. I tried my best to stay with him throughout the race, until the final lap when I noticed he kept looking back to see where I was. The spectators were rooting for him, shouting, "Vefling! Vefling! Vefling!"

Capozzoli was probably too difficult for them to shout. I waited for "Vefling!" to turn his head one more time, and then made a mad dash to pass him, which I did, winning the race in 4:11, a national record, my best mile time ever. The crowd did applaud me, but never did shout, "Capozzoli! Capozzoli! Capozzoli!"

The next day it was a different story. It was the 5,000 meter run against their champion, "Stokken! Stokken! Stokken!" I was so tired from my last three races that I lost my equilibrium, staggered off the track, and ran over a large hose used for watering the track. The spectators laughed. Do they laugh different in Norwegian? The following day the sport's pages read, "Stokken beats Capozzoli!" I finished third.

We then flew onward to Ireland, England, Scotland, and Sweden. In Belfast, Northern Ireland, I ran the three-mile run on a grass track against their champion, John Joe Barry, and won in good time, again convincing my college coach that the longer the distance, the better I was. On this trip, I won five of eleven races. When I arrived home there was a letter that my parents received stating that I had done more for goodwill in Reykjavik, Iceland, than the military could do in weeks. A letter was also received from Dr. George Crane, principal of Bayside High School, who became a good friend, inspired me on, and followed my career.

"Dream! Dream! Dream! Dreams do come true if you believe and work hard to achieve the impossible."

"It's love that really matters!"

Reykjavik, Iceland   July 1951

Ir. 170 - 1951 ————————————————————— ARBEIDERBLADET

Edvin Wide:

«Landskampen burde gi idrettspresse og ledere i Norge en tankevekker»

«Morgon-Tidningen» i Stockholm var representert med den berømte «flygande skol-läraren», Edvin Wide ved fri-idrettslandskampen i Oslo. Det er så mye riktig i hans «sluttinntrykk» at vi siterer:

«Det merkelige har hendt her i Oslo at det svenske B- og C-laget opplevde en virkelig vjemningsfull landskamp. Dette gode har publikum og presse i Oslo i høy grad medvirket til. Den norske hjerteligheten har forekommet meg virkelig påtagelig og klar. Dette er det grunn til å gjenta etter de mange kjølige vindpustene som nå og da har dradd over Kjølen til Sverige årene under og etter den siste verdenskrigen. Som sluttinntrykk fra denne landskamp står det gamle spørsmålet om norsk idrett: Hvordan i all verden er det mulig at den store massen av norske landslagsmenn i fri-idrett er så uskolert og ofte så halvtrent når de inne imellom har slike lysende forbilder snart her og snart der i de forskjellige grenene? Det er nesten så det skjærer i hjertet på en gammel idrettstilskuer når man ser hele rekken av norske praktgutter i landslagsdrakt teknisk sett gjennomføre sine øvelser utrolig klosset. Denne landskampen mot Sveriges B-lag burde ha gitt idrettspresse og ledere i Norge en virkelig tankevekker.»

Når det gjelder de individuelle norske prestasjonene tipper «Morgon-Tidingens» medarbeider Kjærsem som en ypperlig partner for Stokken ved Olympiaden neste år. Av Strandli kan man når som helst vente en verdenssensasjon, og Henry Johansen tør nå være Skandinavias beste sprinter, heter det.

„Vi har ikke bedre baner enn Bislett"

sier Bryan fra California, «men vi har hundrede som er like gode.»

Livfulle amerikanere til Tjalves fri-idrettsstevne

Den neste store fri-idrettsbegivenheten lar ikke vente på seg lenge. Amerikanerne som skal delta på Tjalves stevne mandag og tirsdag ble prestert på landskampens siste dag, like etter at de var kommet til Oslo med fly. Og i går trente de på Bislett.

«Hvordan liker De Bislett» spør vi lengdehopperen Bryan, som ble nr. 2 med 7.45 i matchen USA-Norden på Bislett for 2 år siden.

«Bislett er fin — vi har ikke bedre baner i California — men vi har hundre av dem».

«Men dere kaliforniere er vel svært avhengig av pent vær?».

«Vi vil gjerne ha det slik som det er i dag. Det er ikke varmere i California — men vi har slik varme hele året».

Det er noen kvikke og humørfylte idrettsmenn Tjalve har fått til sitt store stevne, hvor ellers nesten hele den norske eliten starter — og hvor også Sverige visstnok vil bidra til attraksjonen, skjønt det ikke er endelig bestemt hvilke av svenskene vi får se her nå.

McKenley, som er en av neste års olympiafavoritter på 400 meter, vil prøve å bedre sin Bislett-rekord på 46.1. Hans beste resultat er det fantastiske 45.9. Bryan har tidligere 7.74 m. i lengdehopp (det klarer han neppe nå, men han lar seg ikke slå). Chambers har 1,50,4 på 800 m., og Bud Held 73 m. i spydkast. Lille smidige Capozzoli er god for ca. 3,57 på 1500 m., og passer altså bra for norske løpere, som vil ha en amerikansk skalp (hvis de er raske nok i spurten, vel å merke).

«Tjalves amerikanere» har inntatt Bislett. Øverst til venstre Capozzoli (1500 og 3000 m) og Chambers (800 m og 400 ?). Nederst McKinley i mindre anstrengt attityde og innfelt til høyre lengdehopperen Bryan som har gjort 7.74 og 10.6. Hva klarer han nå, mon?

HVA–HVOR–NÅR

26. Juli.

TEVLINGER:
Fotball: Norge—Island i Trondheim.

TRENING:
Volleyballtrening på Bjølsen kl. 19.
Oslo—Odd: Walle Hovind kl. 19.

Hans Andersen inn på Dybwads plass

Norges Fotballforbund meddeler at Gunnar Dybwad, Steinkjer, har meldt forfall til Landskampen mot Island. I hans sted spiller Hans Andersen, Lisleby.

KARR VEFLING LEDER feltet på en engelsk mil. Nærmest følger amerikaneren Capozzoli, deretter Hallgeir Brenden og Knut Tueten.

From European Tour

Charlie Capozzoli, Flushing distance runner, returned home yesterday from a tour of Europe, where he competed in a series of meets with a group of U. S. track and field stars. Here he's greeted by his mother, Mrs. Tanella Capozzoli, and his grandfather, Charles Riccio. Charlie, former Bayside High star attends Georgetown University.

Onsdag 1. august 1951

jår: Stokken 14.23.8 på 5000 meter

400 METER HEKKELØP
gikk som første øvelse, og lovende Arne Engebretsen, Liv, lå lenge først, men maktet ikke avslutningen og havnet på 3. plass. Sterke Hans Egelund, Bestum seiret på 57.1, mens Saxhaug fikk 2. plass på 57.7.

I lengdehoppgropen dalte i mellomtiden amerikaneren Bryan ned på 7.13 tross skadet kne, mens hverken Vikan eller Rune Nilser. kom opp på 7 metern.

1500 m-feltene gikk med «fullt hus», og i A-klyngen kilte Ragnar Haglund, Sarpsborg seg til slutt fram i spissen og vant på 3.57.4, tross mange ytterkurver. Lunås smatt inn på 2. plass, foran hardt kjempende Reidar Hannestad, men begge fikk samme tid. Bjørn Bogerud og Hallgeir Brenden fulgte deretter, også på samme tid, så man forstår at knivingen må betegnes som prima.

B-finalen tok Leif Bjerklund, Vidar hånd om med 4.05.2, og i C-klassen kom Einar Vigerust, NLH først i mål på 4.14.

Stein Johnsen viste seg fortsatt noen streker hvassere enn Ivar Ramstad i diskos, og fikk et lengstekast på 47.10 mot Ramstad 46.59. Ramstad er tydelig ikke i slag ennå, og slo «fra hoften». Stein kaster elegant som vanlig, men hurtigheten er ikke stor nok. Det blir for mye «langsom kino» før diskosen sendes ut.

REKORD-LØPET

På 5000 m fikk som nevnt Ernst Larsen beskjed om å dra, og Larsen. Stokken og amerikaneren Capozzoli skilte seg snart ut som tertrio, mens Kjersem valgte den uheldige taktikk å lede neste klynge, med Tveten på hjul. Denne bommert, som uten tvil må føres på «manglende selvtillits konto», belastet sikkert Kjersem med ekstra 8 sek. i sluttid.

Da 6 runder sto igjen, gikk Larsen ut, Capozzoli hang med til svingen, men plutselig rykket Stokken voldsomt og ristet amerikaneren av seg i en jafs. 3000 m-tiden lød på 8.34, så opplegget lovet bra. Stokken holdt farten, mens Capozzoli slapp mer og mer, og Kjersem synet sjansen, hjulpet fram av publikums-brølene. I hard avslutning brøt Stokken målsnoren på ny norsk rekord: 14.23.8, mens Kjersem i mellomtiden smatt forbi Capozzoli som resignerte, og tressfjordingen gikk inn på fin personlig rekord: 14.38.6. Amerikaneren fikk også ny «pers» med 14.43.6, likeledes Tveten med 15.08.2. Men én ting gleder vi oss til: Nytt samløp mellom Stokken og Kjersem, der «vesle-Jakob» tør være med helt fra begynnelsen . . .

Vi presenterer drabantene som kriget på 5000 m. Fra venstre: Jakob Kjersem, amerikaneren Charles Capozzoli, og lengst til høyre Martin Stokken som satte ny norsk rekord med 14.23.8.

To årsrekorder i Sarpsborg

Stokken 8.28.0 — Boysen 1.52.1

— Privat til Arbeiderbladet —
Sarpsborg, i går.

Det internasjonale fri-idrettsstevnet her i dag bød på en rekke gode resultater, tross en sjenerende vind. Martin Stokken og Audun Boysen satte nye årsrekorder, og Stein Christensen, Kjell Mangset og Bjørn Hansen viste pålitelig form.

Under 100 meter-løpet blåste det medvind, og en må ta dette i betraktning når en vurderer tidene. På 400 meter derimot var vinden avgjort en handicap.

Audun Boysen laget et strålende løp, etter åpning på 53.8. Han ble forbigått av Chambers først i oppløpet.

Martin Stokken og Capozzoli hadde et friskt oppgjør på 3000 meter. Amerikaneren gikk opp og tok ledelsen i tredje runde, men måtte senere se Stokken gå forbi. Capozzoli satte ny personlig rekord.

Resultatene:
110 meter hekk: 1) Bryan, USA, 15.0. 2) Helge Christensen, Viking, 15.3.

1500 meter: 1) Reidar Hennestad, Viking, 0.00.6. 2) Ragnar Haglund 4.00.8. 3) Hallgeir Brenden, Tjalve, 4.01.6.

100 meter: 1) McKenley, USA, 10.4. 2) Bryan, USA, 10.6. 3) Kjell Mangset, Sarpsborg, 10.8. 4) Henry Johansen, Oslo-Ørn, 10.9.

100 meter kl. B: 1) Egil Hansen, Tjalve, 11.0.

Diskos: 1) Stein Johnsen, Tjalve, 48.23.

400 meter: 1) McKenley, USA, 48.0. 2) Bjørn Hansen, Moss, 50.7. 3) Leif Ekeheien, Tjalve, 51.7.

800 meter: 1) Chambers, USA, 1.51.7. 2) Audun Boysen, Torodd, 1.52.1. 3) Sigurd Roll, Ready, 1.59.6.

Spyd: 1) Bucheld, USA, 68.88. 2) Odd Mæhlum, Hamar, 62.87.

Høyde: 1) Bjørn Gundersen, Elverum, 1.90.

3000 meter: 1) Martin Stokken, Selsbakk, 8.28.0. 2) Capozzoli, USA, 8.30.8. 3) Fredrik Eckhoff, Tjalve, 9.03.6.

1000 meter stafett: 1) USA 2.00.0. 2) Sammensatt lag 2.03.1. 3) Tjalve 2.04.0.

Athletic Director
Keflavik, Iceland
July 24, 1951

Dear Mr and Mrs Capozzoli,

This is rather an unusual letter in so much as it concerns your son.
I had the high honor of seeing your boy run in several events here in
Europe and I do want you to know of excllent sportsmanship conduct. For
a young American of his type we are more than proud. You folks I am sure
can be proud. He captured along with all of the races, the fancy of the
fans and people and youngesters here in Iceland. I am sure you would like
to know all about the events.

Charley participated in the 3000 meters and the 1500 meter competition.
Winning both easily the crowd were amazed of his size and ability. We Americans here were more than surprised. The team won all of the events in Iceland and departed this morning for Norway where I know Charles will give a
good account of his ability. The children here were very fond of him and
for several days he was busy signing autographs.

I hope to be in New York soon and probably could give you a better
awcount of the competition. I haven't written to any of the familiES of
the other boys because its a time consuming job. But in this little note
I do want you to know you have reason to be proud of your son. He certainly
is a fine gentleman and sportsman. In this one track meet he has accompolished
more for America thn any of us could ever do in weeks. We express our full
thanks and appreciation to you folks for such a fine Ameriaan son.

My best wishes for his contineous success.

Sincerely,

Michael J Crisci Jr.
Athletic Director
Keflavik, Iceland

Capozzoli Envoy of Good Will

By DON RODDA

Fresh from a European tour with an AAU track and field squad, Charley Capozzoli is back in Flushing for a rest preparatory to resuming activity at Georgetown University.

During his recently-concluded excursion to Scandinavian countries and the British Isles, Capozzoli won five races of 11 entered. He set new national records in Iceland, Northern Ireland and Norway.

In Oslo, the ex-Bayside High School miler defeated the Norwegian champion, Karl Vefling in the mile. Charley turned in a 14:13.2 clocking in the three-mile race in Northern Ireland where he beat John Joe Barry to the tape. And his 8:47 for the 3,000 meters at Reykjavik set a new Icelandic standard.

Among other souvenirs of Charley's five-week tour, his parents, Mr. and Mrs. Joseph Capozzoli today are displaying a letter they received from Michael Crisci, Jr., Athletic Director at Keviavik, Iceland.

Crisci praised Capozzoli's performance and sportsmanship during his running the 3,000 and 1,500 races in Iceland. He wrote:

"In the one track meet, he (Charley) has accomplished more for good international relations than any of us could do in weeks . . . we express our thanks and appreciation to you folks for a fine American son.

Running in Iceland, Norway, Sweden, Scotland, England and Northern Ireland, Capozzoli placed in all but one of his 11 events.

Upon his return to Georgetown next week, Charley will commence training for the indoor track season, during which he expects to enter the lists against Fred Wilt and other topnotchers. Figuring his European tour has put him in excellent shape for future events, the 20-year-old Flushingite hopes he'll be able to repeat some of his schoolboy accomplishments.

As one of George Wright's Bayside runners, Capozzoli won the city and state one-mile champion-

Charlie Capozzoli, former Bayside High track star, and his proud mother read framed letter sent to Capozzoli's parents after the Georgetown University runner won the mile race during an AAU tour of Kevlavik, Iceland. Charlie set a record in winning that race and won the praise of Michael Crisci, Kevlavik athletic director.

ships prior to his graduation in 1949.

At Georgetown, Charley is coached by Frank Sevigne, who has been bringing him along carefully in view of Capozzoli's meager dimensions. Cap, who stands a slim 5-feet-8¼, weighs only 126 pounds. Still, the wiry youngster has been able to hold his own in collegian ranks.

Capozzoli is in his junior year at Georgetown, where he is studying business administration.

Ameriska íþróttamennirnir á æfingu í íþróttavellinum. Talið frá vinstri: Charles Capozzoli, Franklin Held, Gaylord Bryan, Herbert McKenley og Robert Chambers.

Capozzoli Track Champ Of Ireland; Tops Barry

by Tommy Doyle

On July 17, Coach Frank Sevigne, Charley Capozzoli and an assemblage of nation-wide athletes took off via Pan American Airlines for a tour that was to bring prestige, honor and good will to the competitors, coaches and countries. Mr. Sevigne, having coached one of Georgetown's greatest track teams, was invited through the good grace of the Icelandic A.A.U. and thus coached their track team for the six weeks he was over there. Coach Sevigne could have also traveled on the European tour but due to some previous engagements had to decline the offer.

Along with Capozzoli on this trip were such leading track men as: Herb McKinley, the 440 yard world record specialist from Jamaica, West Indies; the former Yale great, Jim Fuchs and the Californian Bud Held, who broke the American record for the javelin throw with a heave of 249 feet in Stockholm, Sweden. With all these stars in the troupe, few were perhaps as successful or sensational as the Long Island boy, Charley Capozzoli. Having entered eleven races, Charley won five, finished up twice in the second slot and twice in the third position. Charley now holds to his credit, the Irish three mile, which he won in Belfast over John Joe Barry, the 1500 and 3000 meters in Iceland; the one mile in Oslo, Norway and finally the one mile in Birmingham, England. In Scotland, during one of the meets, over 80,000 people attended the event. Many fans, who all stood up during the course of the meet, passed out from exhaustion and thus were carried off from the field. The short time between the events was filled with other activities such as: Soccer, bicycle races and football games, though not as we know the game.

Among some of the awards that Charley received were; wrist watches, cigarette cases and lighters, a table lamp, a sheepskin, an Irish linen table cloth, a set of sterling silver tablespoons and a slew of medals and trophies. Charley sacrificed much to make this trip but it is certain that both he, his family and the coach of the boys, Mr. Littlefield from the University of Texas, are proud of his accomplishments

TRIBUTE TO CHARLEY

Because of the fine competitive spirit shown throughout the tour by Cappie an Athletic Director for the Armed Forces was inspired to write a letter to Charley's parents. To quote a few lines, . . . "In this one track meet, He (your son, Charley) has done more good for International Relations than we could do in weeks. Charley captured the fancy of the crowd with his track ability and after each of his events, he was crowded by those seeking autographs. We thank you for having such a fine son." This is only a caption from the genuine copy but it demonstrates the pleasure these people took in watching Charley perform.

LA PIERRE ACTIVE

Most of the boys on the Hoya's track team were working or at Summer School, but Joe Lapierre also made some news with some terrific races. He turned in a 4:10.4 mile in Seattle and a 4.11.6 mile in Buffalo, which is really "burning up the track". Joe could have gone on the European tour along with Charley but turned it down.

Hoya track star, Charley Capozzoli, competed last summer in international track meets.

CAPOZZOLI WINS INTERNATIONAL TRACK HONORS

Last summer, while many of us were filling in courses at SFS, basking in the sun at Santa Monica, or counseling kids in the Catskills, Charley Capozzoli, '53, was winning new track honors all the way from the Pacific coast to the fringes of the Iron Curtain countries in Europe.

After school closed in June, Charley headed for the west coast, where he spent a week in Seattle, and a week in Berkeley, as Georgetown's representative on the National Track Team. Following a short vacation at home in Long Island, he then left for Europe, where he spent four weeks with the U.S. Track Team. This itinerary took him to six western European nations.

It would appear that Americans stationed in Iceland are happy to see Americans from home, for the Commanding General of U.S. Forces there was on hand to greet the team in person, as their plane landed at Reykjavik Airport. Charley said that service personnel were enthusiastic spectators at the meets which followed. Probably the outstanding social event, he recalls, was a dinner given by the Commanding General before the group left for the continent. After leaving Iceland, the team stopped at Oslo, Stockholm, Glasgow, Liverpool, London, Birmingham, and Belfast. Generally speaking, the American team compared favorably with their European contenders, although Charley thinks the English milers are exceptionally good, and the Swedish distance runners outstanding.

Charley took first place in five of the eleven events in which he participated, second in two more events, and in two others he placed third. Among the events in which he placed first, were the 1500 and 3000 meter races in Iceland, the one-mile in Oslo, the one-mile in Birmingham, and the three-mile in Belfast.

57

Board of Education of the City of New York

Bayside High School
208TH STREET AND 32ND AVENUE
BAYSIDE, BOROUGH OF QUEENS, 61
GEORGE J. CRANE, PRINCIPAL

Dr. George J. Crane

September 11, 1951

Mr. Charles Capozzoli
163-17 25th Avenue
Flushing, New York

Dear Charlie:

After a most interesting sabbatical that drew
me to Miami, the Bahamas, Europe, and Cape Cod, I have
returned to Bayside to remain here till the end of this
month. I plan to retire from the Board of Education on
October 1st.

One of the most pleasant surprises awaiting me
was the notice containing your picture and that of your
lovely mother, and the most interesting account of three
European records that you broke.

I am sure, Charlie, that your eleven races across
the pond, five of which you won, have put you in splendid
shape for the most successful track year of your very successful life. Among the thousands of your well-wishers,
there has never been anyone more interested in you and in
your many accomplishments than I. I pray God that the
forthcoming year will be to date the most happy and successful of your life, both scholastically and athletically, and
I do hope you can find the time to visit me at Bayside between now and the end of the month.

Please remember me kindly to your mother, and
rest assured that Mrs. Crane joins me in this expression
of congratulation and respect to one of Bayside's best.

Very cordially yours,

GEORGE J. CRANE
Principal

Thursday, October 25, 1951   *THE HOYA*

The Sporting Thing

by CHARLIE STEELE

There once were two giants who were feared by many men. One of these giants was about ten years older than the other, and, as it happened, died six years before the reputation of the younger was known about the world. Both were from the same small tract of land, however, and both roamed far over the lands, spreading awe and wonder wherever they went.

The older giant could throw a heavy weight farther than any man that had ever lived, and he accomplished this feat many times. Often large crowds would gather to watch, and the people would marvel at his strength. His body was as perfect as could be imagined. He was tall, with bronze skin that fit closely over powerful, rippling muscles.

But this giant could do more than throw heavy weights. He was as fast as the deer, and had the co-ordination of a magnificent time piece.

Every week during the Autumn of the year, many giants competed in a game to see who had the most strength, skill and courage. According to those who knew, this giant was the best of all! at this game. In fact, he was captain, elected by his fellow athletes.

Then one day the country of this giant was attacked by evil men, and this giant led some of his countrymen against the invaders, but he died while fighting for what he believed to be right. A patriot of the highest order, he died for his country. Knowing that he fought on the side of justice and right, he died for his God.

Now the second giant was, by some people's standards, no giant at all. He was only about five feet nine inches tall, and his body was slender. But in spirit he was every bit as much a giant as the older. He could run faster, for greater distances, than anyone for thousands of miles around. From the days of his earliest manhood, this slight, dark-haired giant amazed all who saw him.

There was no attack upon the homeland of this giant during the period with which our story deals, but there was great danger of such an attack. (In this time the giant traveled far and wide, winning friends for his country in this time of danger.) And though this giant was small, he too was a leader of men, and all knew that if the need arose, he could be counted upon. No one doubted the courage or questioned the fighting heart of this young giant.

He prayed to his God each night. He received his God in his heart each morning. He lived so as to be prepared to meet his God at any moment.

The point of the story is this. Georgetown should be proud of these two giants. Because the older was Al Blozis, and the younger is Charley Capozzoli. In the important sense of the word, both are among the biggest of men.

"Frank Sinatra, Coconut Grove, Ambassador Hotel!"

Back in the early 50's, the Ambassador Hotel, a five-star plus, maybe ten stars, was tops in California. It was absolutely beautiful, located on Wilshire Boulevard in Los Angeles. The famous "Brown Derby" was across the street from the hotel.

This happened in my sophomore or junior year. While our coach was checking us into the hotel, in walks Frank Sinatra! Wow! Frank Sinatra! The Sinatra that I admired (singing and bow ties) so much as a child, eight years ago. Maybe he'll listen to me sing the scale, "do, re, mi," as I did for my dad when I was 12 years old and wanted to be a singer like Sinatra and Perry Como. Four of us trackmen, being dressed up the same in Georgetown blue blazers, grey flannel pants, white shirts, and striped dark blue/red ties, were standing in the lobby. Mr. Sinatra approached us and asked why we were staying at the hotel. He may have thought we were bell hops the way we were dressed. We explained that we were "track and field athletes" and going to compete the next day at the Coliseum.

Frank Sinatra was very personable. He spoke to us and to our coach, Frank Sevigne, quite awhile. Our coach was handsome and looked a little like Alan Ladd, a famous movie star in those days. Mr. Sinatra then asked if we had plans for the evening. Our plans were to have an early dinner and then go to our beautiful room to rest. Sinatra told us that he would be performing that evening at the "Coconut Grove," his opening night, and would like for us to be his guests. We accepted his invitation!

Wow! We couldn't believe this was happening to us. Who cared about tomorrow's race? As we arrived at the "Coconut Grove," we were greeted by the maitre 'd who escorted us to a table up front. There were movie stars all over the place. Since there were four of us dressed the same in our traditional Georgetown outfits, everyone must have thought we were a singing quartet, with our handsome coach as the lead singer. Once Sinatra's performance was over, Sinatra joined his guests (the movie stars), and so did I! I went from table to table meeting movie stars, introducing myself as a special guest of Frank Sinatra. What a night it was! Who could sleep after that? I can't remember how we did the next day in the track meet. Our coach then decided that he would no longer put us up at such fancy hotels in the future.

"Miss Universe Contestants!"

That same year, 1951 or 52, we returned to California to compete in the National AAU Championships. After our experience at the Ambassador Hotel, our coach picked out what he thought would be a nice quiet hotel in Long Beach. As we're checking in at the front desk, there was a big commotion outside the hotel. We went out to see what was going on. A "Parade of Cadillac's," Cadillac convertibles, one after another, pulled up in front of the hotel, each with a beautiful lady.

Did our coach know that the hotel we were staying at was also where the "Miss Universe Contestants" would stay? As they entered the hotel lobby, I worked the elevator, taking them up to their floor. I didn't carry their luggage, but would have. Oh! Were these girls beautiful. The next morning at breakfast, "Miss Italy" was sitting at the table across from us. We couldn't help but stare at her and the girls with her. Suddenly "Miss Italy" pointed to me and said something in Italian in a loud and excited voice. I flipped out thinking she wanted to meet me. Then, I was brought back to my senses. The reason she pointed to me was to tell the waiter she wanted what I was drinking, "orange juice," but didn't know how to say it in English.

The excitement and fun didn't end here. One of our team-mates, Dave Boland, rented a Cadillac convertible the next day. As the parade of Cadillac's pulled up in front of the hotel that morning, he joined in, picked up one of the contestants, and followed the other Cadillac's to their destination. Our coach finally gave up in trying to find quiet hotels in the future. We were glad he did! I don't remember how we performed at this track meet either, but we sure had lots of fun. Never did I think being a track athlete would offer so much fun and laughter. We were amateurs, didn't make money, but had the greatest times that one could imagine.

"Turin, Italy, another fun (embarrassing) episode"

Our coach, Frank Sevigne, had nothing to do with this, since I was touring with the USA track team. Made three trips to Europe during the summers of 51, 52, and 53, all expenses paid. After competing during the day in Turin, Italy, we were invited that night to a social gathering for dinner and entertainment. Would you believe it? A beauty contest was taking place! We were introduced to the girls, Italian beauties. I took a liking to one of them (maybe all of them!) and followed her around all evening until someone told me that she was waving "goodbye" to me, instead of asking me to go along with her. The way she was waving, I thought she wanted me to follow her. Oh, well, at least I felt wanted for awhile. Ha! Ha! Who would have ever believed that running would lead to this.

"It was innocent fun, memories that last a lifetime, like treasures of gold"

The Hoya Speedsters

RECORD BREAKING THINCLADS

The Georgetown track team again proved to be the most consistent of the school's sporting teams with another brilliant season. Beginning with the numerous outings of the cross-countryites and carrying through the outdoor season, the Hoyas proved their caliber against the best opposition in the country.

The cross-country season again brought into prominence the name of Charlie Capozzoli, who finished first in all of the dual meets and climaxed the year by placing third in the IC4A meet in New York's Van Courtland Park. The cross-country team emerged victorious in all but one of its dual tussles.

It was the indoor season, however, that was destined to again spray national recognition on the Hoya thinclads. With Racely Saunders combining with returning members of last year's record-breaking team, Dave Boland, Carl Joyce, and Joe La-Pierre, the two mile team took on all comers and again proved to be the best in the land. The tracksters were also successful in their individual encounters. LaPierre's 4:11.2 mile in his first indoor outing; Joyce's second straight victory in the Lapham 1,000-yard event; Saunder's first in the Baltimore 1,000-yard; and Boland's top showings in the 600 were the highlights of the year.

Carl Joyce, Joe LaPierre, Dave Boland, and Charlie Cappozolli, hoya non-pareils

World Record "2" Mile Relay
Georgetown's Greatest

7TH RECORD FALLS TO RELAY

The unbeaten and unbeatable Georgetown two mile relay team of Dave Boland, Joe LaPierre, Carl Joyce and Deady sped to their eighth consecutive win and seventh consecutive record as they circled the oval in 7:40.3.

The Hoyas bettered by almost seven full seconds the meet mark of 7:47.1 set by Seton Hall's world record team in 1942. They had, however, no chance at the world indoor mark since the track measures 12 laps to a mile, smaller than the customary board tracks used in Madison Square Garden and elsewhere.

The Washington baton boys led from the gun to the tape. Dave Boland, running as usual in lead-off position, broke at the head of the field and handed the stick to LaPierre with fifteen yards over Pitt. LaPierre increased it to fifty on the second leg and Carl Joyce with the fastest time of the night, 1:52.9, added another fifty before passing to anchorman Deady. Deady had increased the lead to over 125 yards when he finally broke the tape. In second was Indiana with the Big Ten champs, Michigan, in third.

—Star Staff Photos

JOE DEADY.

DAVE BOLAND.

RUN TO WIN

"Action Speaks Louder Than Words!"

When it comes to running, or any other sport, "Action Speaks Louder Than Words!" In the case of a "track man," it's that moment when you're on the starting line, your stomach has "butterflies" (not real ones), and you're praying to do your best. "On your marks, get set, go!" The starter's gun blasts away. Suddenly the "butterflies" are gone, you're on your way, breathing heavy, your brain is going a mile a minute, faster than any of today's mega computers, and there's one clear thought in your mind, "do your best!" Win or lose, it's doing your best. No excuse for not winning matters. The one who crosses the tape first is declared the winner. That person receives the trophy and the glory.

Do you give up when you've practiced hard, spent years of training, gave up lots of other things, but didn't win the race of your life, or the dream of being number one? Most certainly not! Never give up! Patience and perseverance are the key ingredients that champions are made of. You may not win today, but there's tomorrow, and another tomorrow, and another tomorrow. One of those tomorrow's will be your "today!," the day you win the race you've trained so hard for.

Following pages show Georgetown Men in action. Coach Frank Sevigne and Manager Chuck Boyle led the pack in guiding these men to victory. The ones who never will be forgotten are Al Blozis, Jim Fielding, Carl Joyce, Joe La Pierre, and others. How I admired them for their determination. Then, there's the great, Joe Deady, an amazing runner who later became a coach. Ed Kirk, top miler, who became a pilot in the military, then an executive for a phone company, Vince Kelly who became a doctor, and Pete Fedack who became an attorney. The lists of "Men In Action" doesn't end here. It continues on with today's and tomorrow's Georgetown greats.

"Win or lose, it's doing your best that really matters."

Charlie Capozzoli

FRANK SEVIGNE
Track Coach

TRACK

EORGETOWN's cross-country team came through with an undefeated season. The G.U. harriers conquered LaSalle, Baltimore Olympic Club, Loyola (Balt.), and Virginia. Jim Rams broke the record at A.A.U. meet at Virginia. Members of the cross-country team were: Rams, Smith, O'Brien, Deady, Boland, Michaelides, Dongelewicz, and Kane.

Coach Frank Sevigne came up with some pleasant surprises for G.U. track followers in this his first year at the Hilltop. His pride and

1950 Track Team

Two-Mile Relay Team: Deady, Smith, Boland, O'Brien

66

Carl Joyce   *Mile Relay Team: Hurst, Cino, Boland, Kane*   *Jim Nawn*

joy was the two-mile relay team of: O'Brien, Boland, Smith, and Deady, which set a new meet, new Boston, Garden, and new All-Time Boston Record in the B.A.A. games with a race of 7:41.1.

Bill Mitchell in the hurdles, and his prize dash men: Jim Fielding and Don Stonehouse also furnished Sevigne with some satisfaction

Two-mile relay team in practice

IC4A Cross-Country Championships at Cortlandt Park, N.Y.   *Two-mile relay "on mark" in Evening Star Meet*

at times, along with the mile relay team: Lynch, Kane, Hurst, and Cino.

At the Washington Star Meet Don Stonehouse set a new meet record when he copped the D.C. A.A.U. 100-yd. dash in 10 seconds flat. Jim Fielding also won the 100-yd. dash in 9.8. seconds. Mitchell finished third behind Gehrdes and Morrow. The relay teams both finished second.

Neil Ruddick

At the Boston K. of C. games Fielding won the 50-yd. dash in 5.5 seconds. Mitchell was third in the 45-yd. hurdles.

At the Millrose games the two-mile relay team finished second behind Yale, and Mitchell was fourth in the hurdles.

Bill Mitchell

The two-mile relay team added the N.Y. A.C.; the National A.A.U.; and the IC4A meets to its list of conquests, before a dropped baton broke their string in New York's K. of C. Meet.

Vin Cino

CREDIT: I.N.S. Soundphoto

Jim Fielding, of G.U. (second from left) winning 50-yd. dash at Boston's K. of C. Meet. (Peters of Indiana is second; Kaplan of N.Y.U. third.)

Joe Deady

Georgetown's Greatest

Below—Time out for relaxation!! The World Record 2-Mile Relay Team—Carl Joyce, Dave Boland, Joe Deady, and Joe LaPierre—George Shearing was being featured on the turntable as these Hoya track greats rested between practices.

HOYA Photo—Harold Briggs

Dave Boland and Joe Deady read the HOYA'S story on the NYAC games in last week's issue. It was at this meet that Deady retired with the Matt Halpin Half Mile Trophy.

At the Studies

Carl Joyce explains to Joe LaPierre that everything in school is not

Deady Sets Record In IC4-A '1000'

He Runs 2:11.7; Manhattan Wins Meet, Hoyas Third

By Jack Walsh
Post Reporter

NEW YORK, Feb. 24—Georgetown Captain Joe Deady broke the only I.C.4-A. record with a brilliant 2:11.7 performance in the 1000-yard run but the Hoyas couldn't get any better than third for the team title of the thirtieth indoor championships in Madison Square Garden tonight.

A crowd slimmed to 6110 saw representatives of 45 schools give it the old college try.

With a victory in the two-mile relay, the usual Georgetown specialty and a fourth in the broad jump, Manhattan won the meet with 29 points.

Despite Andy Stanfield's winning jump of 24 feet 5½ inches, shortly after midnight, his Seton Hall team had to be content with second place with 37 2/7 points.

Georgetown, without a single point in the field events, was third with 22.

Gehrmann Beats Wilt Again

In the Lou Zamperini invitation mile, Don Gehrmann won his thirty-ninth consecutive mile and continued his mastery over Fred Wilt, but he couldn't brag over it much. Wilt, sentimental favorite of the crowd, was nipped in a photo at the wire by the strong-finishing Wisconsin grad. It was so close both were timed in 4:08.6.

Wilt, the G-man who runs for New York A. C. but who usually is trailed until the payoff lap by Gehrmann, ran his usual race. Gehrmann had had the kick even if it was by the margin of his track shirt.

A gallant two-mile effort by 110-pound Charlie Capozzoli got Georgetown its last four points The tiny soph held off Army's Dick Shea until the last two laps and Shea captured the grind in 9.12. Capozzoli, who's been training the best distance runners all year, made his best finish of the season in 9.15.9 for second place .

HOYA SETS RECORD—Joe Deady of Georgetown University wins the 1000 yard | final in the IC-4A track meet in New York last night in record-breaking time of 2:11.7

Capozzoli and Deady Make New Records

A magnificent performance by Georgetown's crack track team, as they drew the curtain on the 1951 indoor season, highlighted the 14th annual running of the Cleveland Knights of Columbus Games.

A crowd of 7,900 cheered the Hoyas to two new meet records, Joe Deady in the 1000 yd. run and the undefeated two mile relay team. In addition, they were given an unexpected treat when Charlie Capozzoli, a late entry not listed on the program, wheeled around the track to win the two mile run in 9:08.8, fastest collegiate two mile of the year.

DEADY CRACKS FIRST MARK

The first record of the evening fell to the fleet feet of brilliant Joe Deady, captain and anchorman of the two mile relay team.

In defeating Lawton Lamb, last year's champion and winner at Milwaukee, high stepping Deady was clocked in 2:11.1, bettering by one tenth of a second the former mark of 2:11.2 established by the late John Borican, world record holder for the event, in 1942. It also bettered by six tenths of a second the previous fastest indoor time of the year set by Deady when he won the IC4A championship three weeks ago.

He was not in trouble at any time during the race. He broke in third position but grabbed the lead after the first lap and held it all the way with Lamb approximately three yards behind him. Far arear of Deady and Lamb was third place Don Makielski of Michigan State, and Alex Perrot of Syracuse.

NEW MEET RECORD for the 1000-yard run is hung up by Georgetown's Joe Deady as he breaks the tape three yards in front of Lawton Lamb of Illinois.

LAPPING THE FIELD with the lone exception of Purdue's Denis Johansson (right) is Charley Cappazoli, Georgetower sophomore who won the two-mile run. Johansson still has lap to go as Press Photographer Louie Moore, who took all these Arena pictures, shoots his flashbulb.

CAPPY GREAT

Despite the record breaking performance of Deady and the 2-milers, the crowd got their biggest thrill out of "Added Starter" Capozzoli. The 119 lb. sophomore lapped the entire field with the exception of one man, the Finnish Olympic runner Denis Johansson, now a freshman at Purdue. He failed to catch Johansson by two feet.

Cappy was clocked in 9:07.8, fastest of any collegian so far this year. By his performance he gained the 2nd leg on the Columbian trophy. Curt Stone, last years champ was clocked in 9:14.4

CHARLIE CAPOZZOLI.

71

Charlie Capozzoli

BERKELEY DAILY GAZETTE ... Tuesday Evening, June 19, 1951

Track's Great Gathering Here

Early arrivals for the week end's American track and field championships included entries from two neighboring Eastern seaboard schools, Morgan State and Georgetown University. Morgan State's trio, left, was anxious to test the Edwards Stadium cinders even before changing to their track togs for a workout at 3 o'clock yesterday afternoon. Left to right are George Rhoden, defending 400-meter champion; Art Bragg, 100-meter titlist, and quartermiler Sam LaBeach. Rhoden and Bragg compiled 38 points in the short races to earn the Baltimore school third place in Saturday's NCAA meet. Georgetown's aces, Joe Deady, left, and Charles Capozzoli, go in for longer events. Deady anchored the Hoyas' two-mile relay quartet to a mark under the existing world record at the Coliseum Relays and placed sixth in the NCAA 880. Capozzoli was second in the NCAA two-mile.
—Gazette photos

72

Chapter 9
"Junior Year at Georgetown"

After returning from Europe, I spent a few weeks at home enjoying the family, especially mom's cooking. At dinner time, I told them how exciting it was visiting different countries and meeting so many wonderful people. It was hard to imagine that only several years before, World War II took place. In Cologne, Germany, buildings were still in shambles from bombing. I met Germans whom I associated with and loved. The food in Germany provided an excellent diet for athletes, "first the soup (with an egg dropped in it, whirled around while it was boiling). Then, came the lean beef, french-fries, and a nice buttered lettuce salad. In Iceland, it was the salmon just caught out of their icy waters. The breakfast in Norway and Sweden was enough to hold you off for the rest of the day, but after competing, the evening dinner desserts made you think you died and went to heaven. I couldn't help think "what a beautiful world God created." Why do people want to destroy it and one another? In spite of the delicious food I ate in these countries, none could compare to moms. She had the magic touch!

Junior year at Georgetown began with cross-country training, competing against different universities. This was to get us in top condition for the indoor track season that began in January. Cross-country was my cup of tea, winning several races, also getting lost in some. The races were thru woods, "hill and dale." If you were out front leading the pack and unfamiliar with the course, it was possible to miss a directional sign and get lost. This happened to me twice in high school at van Cortland park where years later I set the inter-collegiate "IC4A 5 mile record." I finally knew the course with my eyes closed.

"Don't always obey your coach to follow the leader!"

A cross-country race, in particular, goes down in the history books of screw-ups! It took place in Virginia at a university we never before visited or competed against. Before the race, we were driven in a van and shown where the race began and ended. We were advised to follow the directional signs, the pointed arrows, thru-out the woods. Our coach advised my team-mates, "follow Capozzoli. Stay as close to him as possible." I had been winning all the cross-country races, setting records in each. The gun went off. I took the lead, setting a fast pace at the beginning to discourage the competition. The late Carl Joyce and Joe la Pierre usually stayed close to me during these races, finishing second and third. They followed me. The race seemed to be getting longer and longer. I was beginning to wonder how far we had to go to the finish. I kept a grueling pace. I turned around to see if anyone was following me because I became concerned that I might be lost. Carl and Joe were about 50 yards behind me, so I kept on going. I came to a chain-link fence, about 8 feet high. Never before did I run a course where one had to climb over a fence. I looked back again. Carl and Joe were in pursuit. I climbed over the fence, crossed a highway, and on to a cornfield, the corn was high and ready for picking. I now knew that I was lost! I stopped, turned around, and began walking back to the highway. Carl and Joe were climbing over the fence. Carl yelled out, "You're lost!"

Hitch a ride!

It's much easier than running, besides we were lost and didn't know how to get back to the university. A black man gave us a ride to the university. As we approached the university, we saw that the race was still going on. We asked the kind gentleman to let us off where no one could see us. We then joined the race. Our fourth man, Tom Voorhees, didn't follow us, nor did he know we were lost.

When he crossed the finish line, our coach quietly said to him, "where the **** is Capozzoli, Joyce, and La Pierre?"

"You mean I won?" Tom responded.

When we finally crossed the finish line, all three of us together, our coach quietly said, "where the **** have you been?"

We began to explain, but he stopped us short.

"Tell me later," he said quietly. They're counting you in the score."

We won the team title. When returning to Georgetown the priest in the confessional couldn't understand what I was trying to confess.

"Here we come, judge!"

Another unforgettable experience also happened in Virginia after a cross-country meet. As we crossed the finish line, a successful Georgetown alumnus gave each of us a ten-dollar bill. In 1951, that was enough for a movie and dinner out in Washington D.C. We were grateful for this money and planned how we would spend it once we returned to Georgetown. As we left Virginia late that night to return to Georgetown, the team was separated into two groups. Several went back with Frank Sevigne, our coach, in his car, and four others drove back with the team manager, Chuck Boyle, in Georgetown's station wagon. Chuck was a great team manager and is a good friend to this day. At first I thought I was fortunate to go back with him, until a sheriff pulled us over for speeding. Chuck told the sheriff that our speeding was nothing compared to our coach's who got a late start and was speeding behind us trying to catch up.

The sheriff didn't buy Chuck's story. "Follow me to the courthouse."

As we followed the sheriff, Chuck said to us, "Put your ten dollars in your shoes," which we did.

When we arrived at the "Justice of the Peace," he had Chuck stand in front of him and issued a fine of about $80.00 to be paid in cash immediately, or else we could not leave to continue on to Georgetown. Chuck pleaded with him explaining that we just competed in a cross-country meet, were Georgetown athletes, and had no money.

The judge wouldn't give in and said, "You will not leave here until you come up with the money!"

Chuck then came to us and said, "take off your shoes and give me your ten dollars, or we'll have to spend the night here."

We took off our shoes in front of the judge, the sheriff, and others, gave him the money, and continued on to Georgetown. We laughed all the way!

Several months later, the indoor season began with the Washington Star Games. I won the two mile run beating some of the best two milers, collegiate and AAU participants. The next race was in Cleveland, Ohio. Georgetown's great half-miler and 1,000-yard champion, Joe Deady, won that night, setting a new meet record and dazzled the crowd. He came back that night and anchored the two-mile relay team (Boland, La Pierre, Joyce, Deady) to another record. He was a great competitor. We are very close friends to this day and hope to see each other soon. He married a wonderful woman, named Emily. She is another great cook. After Joe won, it was now my turn to run against Dennis Johansson of Purdue, the Olympian runner from Finland. It was 24 laps around this track for the two-mile run. I didn't know much about Johansson before the race. I just ran to do my best, "run to win!" Before I knew it, I was out front most of the way, and just missed lapping him as I crossed the finish line. My time was 9:07.8, the fastest time run that year by a by a collegian. This was indoors, whereas my time of 9:04 the year before as a sophomore was outdoors.

More than ever, my college coach was convinced that I was better at distance races. I now began to wonder if he would have me running the marathon?

Once he said to me, and was serious, "You'll never be a great miler."

"How could he say that to me?" I said to myself. "Was he using reverse psychology? I ran a 4:11 mile against Vefling In Norway when I just turned 20 years old. I ran one of the fastest high school miles ever against Fred Dwyer, 4:22.9, both of us only one and seven tenths of a second off the National High School record. My high school coach, and Lou Werner, a physical education teacher at Bayside, thought I could someday run the four minute mile."

"Don't let anyone tell you what you can't do!" Believe in yourself, for nothing is impossible.

"Making the Olympic team!"

In June 1952, the Olympic Trials took place at the Coliseum in Los Angeles. Several Georgetown runners competed in the trials, hoping to make the team. I ran the 5,000 meters on Friday. Fortunately, I came in third, Curtis Stone first, and Wes Santee second. Having made the team, I went to the nearest pay phone (cell phones didn't exist) to call home. Mom answered the phone. She told me that she prayed I would make the team, thinking the race was on Saturday, following day.

I choked up. "Mom! I already made the team!"

There was no reply, only silence.

I thought she fainted or had a heart attack. Finally, she started to speak expressing her happiness.

"Mom! Break the good news to dad and everyone. Love you!"

Having made the team, we were now regrouped and reported to Mr. Brutus Hamilton, the head track coach. As we flew back from Los Angeles to New York, the plane lost altitude over St. Louis. The force of gravity pulled us to our seats with great pressure. One could not stand up if they wanted to. Lindy Remigino, who sat next to me, pointed out the window. We could see we rapidly approached the earth. The pilot was planning to crash land. By the grace of god, one engine started up again, the plane began to ascend, and gained altitude.

Mr. Brutus Hamilton got on the speaker. "We just had a horrible experience, but everything is now okay."

He cautioned us not to mention anything to the sportswriters who waited for our arrival at the airport in New York.

"We still have 7,000 miles to go to Finland. We don't want our families to worry."

My parents were at the airport waiting for me. They asked, "How was the plane trip?"

"Great," I said. (A little white lie?).

"Do what you believe in. Dream the impossible dreams. Don't always follow the leader. Let no one tell you what you can't do!"

Chapter 10
"XV Olympiad, Helsinki, Finland,
July 19th—August 3rd, 1952"

When arriving in New York, after that near disaster plane trip, the Olympic track team spent several days at Princeton University where practice sessions continued before leaving for Helsinki. It meant more hard work. I had already been working my tail off. How much more could I possibly do? I did find that I needed to increase my speed work, running sprints, one after another until my body said, "I've had it!"

Wonderful relationships were formed with other team members, McMillen, Barnes, Remigino, Ashenfelter, Mathias, Santee, O'Brien, Richards, Campbell, Bragg, Wilt, Stone, on and on it goes. How priceless it was to know and associate with these great athletes, many who won Olympic titles, setting Olympic and World records. I couldn't believe I had the honor of knowing them. I became very close with McMillen, Barnes and Remigino. McMillen ran a close second to Jose Bartel in the 1,500 meter-run. Ashenfelter set a steeplechase record. Lindy Remigino shocked the world by winning the 100-meters. I ran the 5,000-meters, shocked no one, coming in seventh in my heat, failing to qualify for the finals.

What a thrill it was to take part in the opening ceremonies. Finally, I was in a parade wearing an attractive USA uniform, marching before thousands of spectators. It brought back memories of my childhood in College Point when I would watch the parades go by in front of dad's shoe shop, wishing that I could someday march in one. Never did I imagine that I would someday march in the biggest parade ever. "Dreams do come true!"

Several days before competition, we practiced in a grassy field outside the stadium. During one practice session, a runner, smaller than I, passed me, running at a good clip. I thought, you can't let this little guy show me up, especially since the coaches, Brutus Hamilton being one of them, are watching us work out.

I ran after this runner, pulled along side and passed him. He then passed me, and the race began. I would pass him, and then he would pass me. I thought, this guy just won't quit.

This went on for about 30 minutes. I actually stopped several times, but knowing the coaches were watching, I started after him again. We finally ended our race, with him beating me. The Olympic coaches then came to me and said that watching us was better than watching the Olympic races.

I didn't find out until later that this runner was "Alan Mimoun," one of the fastest distance runners in the world, only second to Zatopeck. A few days later, Mimoun was in my trial heat, beating me again, and qualifying for the finals. He finished second to Zatopeck in the 5,000 and 10,000 meter run finals. I was seventh in my heat and failed to qualify. See photo.

After competing in our events, it was time to relax, enjoy Finland, and date their beautiful young ladies. Three of us dated and picnicked with three Finnish girls (not athletes). They made lunch that we enjoyed immensely. They spoke a little English. We could not speak any Finnish, but had a great time anyway. I took my date to a movie the following night. While waiting in the lobby for the next matinee to begin, she started twitching. I wondered what was wrong with her. I then found out that other foreign Olympians pinched her "you know where." I was ready to take them on, thinking how disrespectful. I remembered my boxing days in New York when growing up. Fortunately, she stopped me, telling me not to be upset. She explained Europeans, especially the Italians, show their admiration of ladies by pinching them in the "you know where!" She was a lovely young lady. No! I didn't show my admiration the way the others did, even though I was of Italian descent.

The games came to an end. So did my dating this beautiful Finnish girl. The closing ceremony and parade was bigger and more exciting than the opening. It was time to say goodbye to our foreign competitors (friends). The next day, Brutus Hamilton, the head Olympic track and field coach, assembled the team at Olympic village with sports writers attending.

"You are going to be immortal," he said. "You have won all the medals you were supposed to win. You have won others you were not supposed to win. I can't tell you how very happy you have made me. This is my farewell to the troops." He went on to say, "I think if I were to mention anyone as being typical of the fine spirit of this team, it would be Charles Capozzoli. He ran far and away the best race of his life even though he did not score."

Wow! When I heard this I almost wet my pants like I did when my sister Marion was born eleven years ago. Associated press articles appearing in New York read, "Hoyas' Capozzoli, spirit of u.s. team."

This meant a lot to me, but it was never recorded in the Olympic book that followed.

"Do your best, my son, run to win! It's love that really matters, and in our heart it sings. So dream, my son, dream of wondrous things!"

Hoyas' Capozzoli
Spirit of U.S. Team

HELSINKI, July 27 (P).—Brutus Hamilton told the 1952 American track and field team today:

"You are going to be immortal.".

He spoke behind closed doors in a little, spic and span school auditorium near the American camp. His voice was low and charged with emotion.

"You have done a tremendous job," he said. "You have won all the medals you were supposed to win. You have won others you were not supposed to win. I can't tell you how very happy you have made me."

Hamilton, athletic director at the University of California, is head coach. Under the rules he can never serve again.

"This is my farewell to the troops," he said.

At the end of his speech there was long, fervent applause.

Charlie Capozzoli

Hamilton did not try to call the imposing roster of American champions (the United States won 14 of the 24 men's events). Instead he said:

"I think if I were to mention anyone as being typical of the fine spirit of this team it would be Charles Capozzoli. He ran far and away the best race of his life even if he did not score."

Capozzoli, a tiny Georgetown student from Flushing, N. Y., competed in the 5000 meters.

This Certifies that

Charles J. Capozzoli

was selected a member of the track and field   team of

The United States Olympic Team of 1952

Tryouts held at Los Angeles, Cal.

United States Olympic Committee

SECRETARY   PRESIDENT

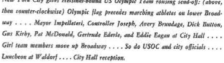

New York City gives Helsinki-bound US Olympic Team rousing send-off: (above, then counter-clockwise) Olympic flag precedes marching athletes on lower Broadway . . . . Mayor Impelleteri, Controller Joseph, Avery Brundage, Dick Button, Gus Kirby, Pat McDonald, Gertrude Ederle, and Eddie Eagan at City Hall . . . . Girl team members move up Broadway . . . . So do USOC and city officials . . . . Luncheon at Waldorf . . . . City Hall reception.

Queens Delegation Headed for Helsinki

Among the U.S. Olympic group taking off for Helsinki today were three Queens girls, who are shown here being wished bon voyage by Charlie Capozzoli of Flushing, who is a member of the men's track squad. Honored in a parade in Manhattan yesterday and greeted by Mayor Impelliterri were (left to right), Capozzoli, Marjorie Larney of Woodhaven, the 15-year-old "baby" of the U.S. team; Mae Faggs of Bayside, who also represented the U.S. in 1948, and Dolores Dwyer of Woodside.

GU'S CAPOZZOLI WINS OLYMPIC TRACK BERTH

Hoya Ace Third In 5,000 Meters

Special to the Times-Herald

Los Angeles, June 27—Charley Capozzoli of Georgetown university today gained a berth on the American Olympic track team by finishing third behind ex-Penn State Curtis Stone and Kansas's Wes Santee in the 5,000 meters finals of the Olympic track tryouts.

Stone, already a team member at 10,000 meters, set a new American record of 14.27 in defeating the hightly regarded Santee and Capozzoli.

THE DISTRICT OF COLUMBIA ASSOCIATION OF THE AMATEUR ATHLETIC UNION OF THE UNITED STATES

XV OLYMPIAD

HELSINKI, FINLAND, JULY 19—AUGUST 3, 1952

Charles J. Capozzoli

Having, in honest competition, won the privilege and responsibility of representing this country in the XV Olympiad at Helsinki, Finland, did, thru superior performance and magnificent sportsmanship bring honor and glory to the United States of America, the City of Washington, and this Association of the Amateur Athletic Union.

PRESIDENT

BY DIRECTION OF THE BOARD OF MANAGERS

SECRETARY

Off for Helsinki, and Uncle Sam's best track and field record in Olympic history.

HAMMER THROW
Final—Won by Martin Engel, N.Y. Pioneer Club, 182 ft. 5 in.; 2—Sam Felton, US Navy, 182 ft.; 3—Bob

50,000 METERS WALK
Leo Sjogren, Finnish-American AC; Adolf Weinacker, Detroit, Mich., and John Deni, Pittsburgh, Pa., selected (See page 71).

52' Olympic' 5,000- meter trial heat.
First five qualify for the final.

I'm now in Helsinki, Finland, on the starting line of the 5,000 meter-run, before a crowd of thousands of people from all over the world. I thought, dreams do come true.

There were many communist' spectators, some athletes in my race. It was a great opportunity to show signs of my faith. Before the gun went off, I made the sign of the cross, proudly professing my faith. I offered up my race for the greater glory of God. The thought of winning, "Run to Win," did come to my mind, but my parents words rang out in my heart, "Do your best, my son. Win or lose, its love that really matters!"

I took the lead, per picture below, setting the pace for most of the thirteen laps when I suddenly became very tired and watched the other runners pass me, leaving me behind. I finished seventh. The first five qualified for the final. While I didn't qualify, I felt good in that I tried my best, which is all I could hope to do.

Olympic Coach Lauds Cappy's Sportsmanship

Capozzoli and Mimoun in the
5,000 Meters Trial Heat

Following is the last lap of the 5,000 meters trial heat. I held the lead for most of the thirteen laps. Gordon Pirie is shown in first place, Alan Mimoun in second, and me in fifth. That's John Landy in front of me in fourth place. Mimoun won, Pirie was fifth, I was seventh and Landy tenth. The first five qualified for the finals. In the finals, It was Zatopek, Mimoun, Shade, Pirie, and Chataway. Mimoun was also second to Zatopek in the 10,000 meters.

"Next Time, Charlie, pick On Your Own Size"

1952 OLYMPIC 5,000 METER RUN FINALS

With 250 meters still to be covered in fast 5000-meters race, Chataway of Great Britain snatches lead from Schade of Germany, with Zatopek of Czechoslovakia and Mimoun of France close behind.

5000-METERS RUN

Emil Zatopek won his second victory of the 1952 Games when he won the 5000-meters and set a new Olympic record of 14:06.6. It was the second time in history that one man has been able to win both the 10,000 and 5,000. Hannes Kohlemainen, famed Finnish runner, did it in 1912. Zatopek failed in this double in 1948 as Gaston Reiff of Belgium beat him by a narrow margin in the 5,000.

Reiff was unable to stay with the pace this time and dropped out at the twelfth lap. Zatopek had plenty of capable opposition, however. Herbert Schade of Germany had set a new Olympic record in his qualifying round and led the field most of the way in the final. Christopher Chataway of Great Britain and Alain Mimoun of France, along with Reiff, were right with Zatopek all the early laps. This was one of the great contests of the XV Olympiad and 70,000 were there to see it.

As the field started out the final 400 meters Zatopek sprinted ahead. Chataway, the gritty Britisher, went right with him and Schade, Mimoun and Gordon Pirie of Great Britain followed. As the bunched fivesome fought it out on the backstretch, Chataway took the lead and Zatopek, Schade and Mimoun pulled away from Pirie. Chataway held it on the turn but as the irresistible Zatopek thundered off the turn to regain the lead, Chataway, in giving challenge, hit the curb, stumbled and fell. He regained his feet but was faltering the rest of the way home. The incredible Czech went to the tape four yards ahead of Mimoun who just beat Schade, Pirie managed to nip his dreadfully tired countryman, Chataway, at the line.

The three American entries, Charles J. Capozzoli, Georgetown University student from Flushing, N.Y., D. Wesley Santee, Kansas University student from Ashland, Kan., and Curtis Stone of

WORLD RECORD: Gunder Hagg, Sweden, 1942—13 min. 58.2 sec.
OLYMPIC RECORD: Emil Zatopek, Czechoslovakia, 1952—14 min. 06.6 sec.
AMERICAN RECORD: Lauri Lehtinen, 1932, and Ralph Hill, 1932—14 min. 30 sec.

Preliminaries

Heat 1	Min.-Sec.
1. A. Mimoun, France	14:19.0
2. I. Taipale, Finland	14:22.8
3. G. Reiff, Belgium	14:23.8
4. A. Andersson, Sweden	14:25.0
5. D. Pirie, Gt. Britain	14:26.2
6. N. Popov, USSR	14:28.6
7. C. Capozzoli, US	14:39.0
8. A. Sutter, Switzerland	14:45.2
9. O. Saksvik, Norway	14:55.4
10. J. Landy, Australia	14:56.4

11. H. Perz, Austria	14:57.2
12. O. Inoue, Japan	14:59.0
13. S. Pavlovic, Yugoslavia	14:59.2
14. J. Kovács, Hungary	17:09.2

Heat 2	
1. H. Schade, Germany	14:15.4
2. A. Parker, Gt. Britain	14:18.2
3. E. Béres, Hungary	14:19.6
4. L. Theys, Belgium	14:22.2
5. E. Toumaala, Finland	14:26.8
6. I. Séménov, USSR	14:28.8
7. A. Graj, Poland	14:30.0
8. O. Cosgül, Turkey	14:36.2
9. B. Karlsson, Sweden	14:45.8
10. P. Page, Switzerland	14:57.0
11. A. Baghanbachi, Iran	15:03.0
12. B. Abdelkrim, France	15:10.2
13. D. Santee, US	15:10.4
14. Z. Ceraj, Yugoslavia	15:17.8

Heat 3	
1. A. Anoufriév, USSR	14:23.6
2. B. Albertsson, Sweden	14:26.0
3. E. Zatopek, Czecho.	14:26.0
4. L. Perry, Australia	14:27.0
5. C. Chataway, Gt. Britain	14:27.8
6. I. Planck, Denmark	14:31.6
7. M. Stokken, Norway	14:39.0
8. C. Stone, US	14:42.8
9. J. Schlegel, France	14:45.6
10. K. Roetzer, Austria	14:49.4
11. V. Koskela, Finland	14:50.8
12. V. Ilic, Yugoslavia	14:51.6
13. P. Frieden, Luxembourg	15:23.2
14. K. Jóhansson, Iceland	15:23.8
15. A. van den Rydt, Belgium	15:51.2

Final	
1. E. Zatopek, Czecho.	14:06.6
2. A. Mimoun, France	14:07.4
3. H. Schade, Germany	14:08.6
4. D. Pirie, Gt. Britain	14:18.0

Rounding final turn in 5000 ... least minutes Chataway ...

1952 0LYMPIC 3,000 METER STEEPLECHASE
ASHENFELTER WINS BREAKING ALL RECORDS

In 3000-meters steeplechase Horace Ashenfelter of US leads in early going . . .

. . . favorite, Kazantsev of USSR, leads later in race . . .

1952 OLYMPIC 100 METER DASH
LINDY REMIGINO WINS

Another angle on much-discussed 100-meters race: (l. to r.) Treloar, Bailey, Smith,
Champion Remigino, Runner-up McKenley, Soukharev.

1952 OLYMPIC 1,500 METER RUN FINALS
BOB McMILLEN A CLOSE SECOND

Barthel's strong drive to new 1500-meters record thwarts McMillen's stirring bid; Lueg is third, Bannister fourth, El Mabrouk fifth.

1500-meters Champion Barthel is moved by strains of his native Luxemburg's national anthem; McMillen, US, is in front, Lueg, Germany, behind.

Picture below of my Olympic buddies, Bob McMillian and John Barnes, who coached me from the sidelines when competing against Gordon Pirie.

MORE NOURISHMENT--Charley Capozzoli, Georgetown 5,000-meter runner; Bob McMillen Occidental College 1,500-meter star, and his teammate, John Barnes, 800-meter fortified at the table.

Chapter 11
"Capozzoli, USA, Versus Pirie, England"

While eating with my Olympic teammates in our compound at Olympic Village, the last gathering before leaving Helsinki, several English athletes passed by.

Gordon Pirie yelled out to me, "Capozzoli! I'm going to whip your *** in London." He, being fourth in the final 5,000 meter run, referred to the British Empire games that were to take place in two weeks.

I didn't know why he said that to me. He beat me in the 5,000-meter heat and ran a good fourth in the finals against Zatopek, Mimoun, and Schade.

I said to my teammates, Bob McMillen and John Barnes, "Why is he picking on me?"

"Don't worry about it." Bob and John said. "When we get to England, we will coach you during the three mile run against him."

I was overwhelmed to think they thought I could beat him. This built up my confidence.

After two weeks of traveling in small towns in Finland, the Olympic team having been broken up into small groups, we now arrive in England. It's time for Gordon Pirie and me to compete.

Before the race, a masseur, my first and only massage ever, said to me, "Oh! Boy! You're going to fly today (did he know about the angels?). Your muscles are fine tuned!"

I now had added confidence, in addition to McMillen and Barnes.

The stadium was packed, 50,000 plus spectators, with

thousands having been turned away. I'm now on the start of the three-mile run against Gordon Pirie and other top English runners. The gun goes off. I don't take the lead as advised by my teammates before the race. I'm told to stay close to the leaders.

"We'll tell you when to go 'full steam ahead'," Bob and John said.

The bell rang for the last lap. I was behind Pirie and Sando.

With 300 yards to go, McMillen and Barnes yelled out, "Go Cappy! Go now!"

I took the lead. The crowd roared! I never turned my head to see where Pirie was. With the crowd yelling, I ran faster than ever, thinking Pirie was going to overtake me. The angels then came into play. I not only crossed the finish line first, but also broke the American outdoor record, in 13:51.8. The New York Herald Tribune read, "he ran faster than Sydney Wooderson's listed British record, faster by twenty-two seconds than Jack Lovelock ran in this meet sixteen years ago."

Brutus Hamilton, head Olympic coach of track and field, was quoted. "Charlie comes as close to maximizing his physical potentialities as any runner I've ever seen."

Pirie and I became close friends from then on. "Next time, Gordon, pick on someone your size!"

We then left England, returned to the good old USA, with my parents anxiously waiting, having a surprise celebration at home with my fan club, Mom, Dad, Lou, Marion, Grandpa, (champeen of da woild!), aunts, uncles, cousins and friends. How wonderful it was to be with those whom I loved so much.

"Dream, my son, dream of wondrous things, for today will soon be over, who knows what tomorrow brings. It's love that really matters!

Charlie Capozzoli, NCAA and IC4A cross country champion,
shown as he set the U.S. National 3-mile record of 13:51.8
in the British Empire vs. U.S. meet at London, August 4.
Doug Pirie and Frank Sando trail. (Courtesy Athletics World)

Capozzoli in Stunning 3 Miles

Another Queens boy, Charley
Capozzoli, Georgetown junior, and
former Public Schools Athlete

He ran faster than Sydney
Wooderson's listed British record,
faster by twenty-two seconds than
Jack Lovelock ran in this meet
sixteen years ago.

"Charlie comes as close to maximizing his physical potentialities,"
said the noblest Roman, Brutus,
"as any runner I've ever seen."

. His Best Race by Far

Capozzoli, of Flushing, L. I., who
had run Wilt off the Olympic
5,000-meter team, ran the fastest
race of his life at Helsinki (14:39)
and failed to qualify. Today he
bettered his best three-mile time
by twenty-one seconds.

What kind of red meat is he
feeding on? "I'm eating fish,"
said fast-time Charley.

"I was determined not to take
the lead," said the I. C. 4-A champion. "I never followed such a
fast pace before, a 5.34 mile, a 9:17
two mile. I felt wonderful. I decided I'd pass Pirie only once but I
waited to make it good. I wonder
what my last quarter was? I hope
my brother and sister see the
papers."

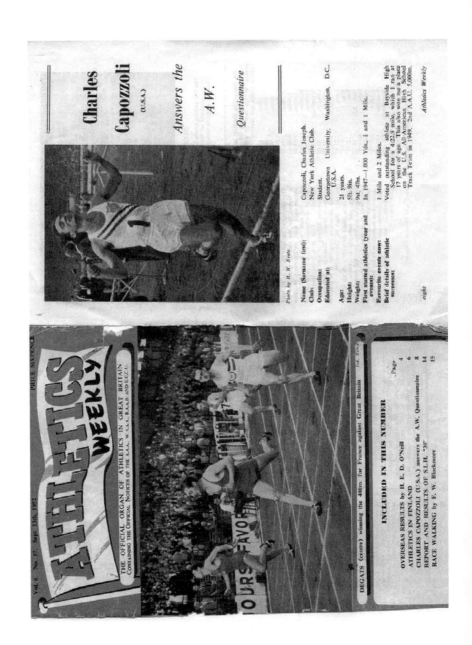

Charles Capozzoli
(U.S.A.)

Answers the

A.W.

Questionnaire

Photo by R. W. Keale

Name (Surname first):	Capozzoli, Charles Joseph.
Club:	New York Athletic Club.
Occupation:	Student.
Educated at:	Georgetown University, Washington, D.C. U.S.A.
Age:	21 years.
Height:	5ft. 9in.
Weight:	9st. 4lbs.
First started athletics (year and event):	In 1947—1,000 Yds., ½ and 1 Mile.
Favourite events now:	1 Mile and 2 Miles.
Brief details of athletic successes:	Voted outstanding athlete at Bayside High School for a 4:22.9 mile, which I ran at 17 years of age. This also won me a place on the U.S. All-American High School Track Team in 1949, 2nd A.A.U. 5,000m.

Athletics Weekly

eight

Vol. 6. No 37. Sep 13th, 1952   PRICE SIXPENCE

ATHLETICS WEEKLY

THE OFFICIAL ORGAN OF ATHLETICS IN GREAT BRITAIN
CONTAINING THE OFFICIAL NOTICES OF THE A.A.A., W.A.A.A., R.A.A.B. AND E.C.C.U.

DEGATS (centre) winning the 400m. for France against Great Britain *1st. News*

INCLUDED IN THIS NUMBER

	Page
OVERSEAS RESULTS by H. E. D. O'Neill	4
ATHLETICS IN FINLAND	6
CHARLES CAPOZZOLI (U.S.A.) answers the A.W. Questionnaire	8
REPORT AND RESULTS OF S.L.H. "20"	14
RACE WALKING by F. W. Blackmore	15

Mae Faggs Sprints to Olympic Win
Capozzoli Smashes U. S. Recorc

Mae Stars With 440 Relay Team In Helsinki Win

By Elizabeth Fitch

The United States of America, New York City, and Bayside are all justly proud of Mae Faggs, Bayside Olympic speedster. Mae graduated from Bayside High School in June, 1952, and in July led the United States Women's Relay Team to victory, at Helsinki, Finland, and since then has been accorded country and city-wide acclaim. These honors have come to Mae after years of perserverance and endurance.

The Bayside track star began her brilliant running career in the spring of 1948. One day at Public School 162 little Mae wandered over to watch Patrolman Al Dykes, then of the 111 Precinct, coach a boys' try-out for a Police Athletic Relay team. Mae asked him to let her run, too, but Dykes refused. The boys, however, persuaded him to change his mind and let her run with them. Mae finished ahead of her male opponents!

No Girls' Team at First

Although no P.A.L. girls' track program was then in existence, Mae ran and trained whenever possible with the boys. In 1947 a P.A.L. track team was organized for girls and Mae was rarin' to go. At this time, a turning point in her career occurred. John P. Brennan of Woodside, former Fordham miler and cross-country track man, and present coach of the Equitable girls' squad recognized in Mae a potentially great athlete and began coaching her. Brennan had to start with racing essentials because Mae had had no previous instructions from a track man. The young speedster began to stand out in Queens P.A.L. and Park Department and other races of the 50 and 60 yard distance.

In 1948, at 16, she became the

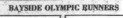

BAYSIDE OLYMPIC RUNNERS

Mae Faggs

Charlie Capozzoli

Dear Charles,

I treasure our association this past summer and I shall always remember your inspired and inspirational performances. I shall follow your career with great interest to the eventual high goal which I'm certain you shall achieve. Every good wish.

Brutus Hamilton

Cappy Rewrite Track Mark Fo Three Mile Run

Charlie Capozzoli, pint sized Bayside graduate, hit the headlines this summer as one of America's top long distance runners. Charlie, who was on the U.S. Olympic team in the 5,000 meter event, performed his greatest athletic achievement to date, after the Olympic games. On August 4, Charli ran three miles faster than any other American in history. It is said that Capozzoli uses more of his potential than any other runner in the world.

Brutus Hamilton, track and field coach of our Olympic team, paid Capozzoli a tremendous compliment when he said, "I think if I were to name anyone as being typical of the fine spirit of this team, it would be Charles Capozzoli. He ran far away the best race of his life, even if he did not score."

Actually, in Olympic competition Charlie failed to qualify for the final finishing seventh in his heat. He was right up with the leaders until the last three laps when he faded and finished 100 yards behind. His time for the 5,000 meters was 14:39.0.

Excels in London

Competing in a post-Olympic dual meet between the U.S. and the British Empire in London, Charlie ran ahead of Curtis Stone and Willia Ashenfelter, both Olympic runners, winning the three mile event in the blazing time of 13:51.8. The brilliance of this feat can be shown by comparing it to the Georgetown senior's performance at the Canadian National Exhibition Track and Field Meet in Toronto. Running the same distance from scratch against a handicap of 350 yards, Charlie won the race in 15:41.8. This time is a full minute 49¼ seconds slower than his London triumph.

Track All-American

Capozzoli, who brought national fame to Bayside High by being selected on the 1949 "Look" magazine All-American high school track team was overshadowed only by the Army's Dick Shea this past winter in the indoor collegiate long distance races. Charlie ran second to Shea in the IC4A two mile event as well as many of the other indoor shows. However his London effort ranks better than Greg Rice, Glen Cunningham, Gil Dodds, and all other Americans in the three mile event.

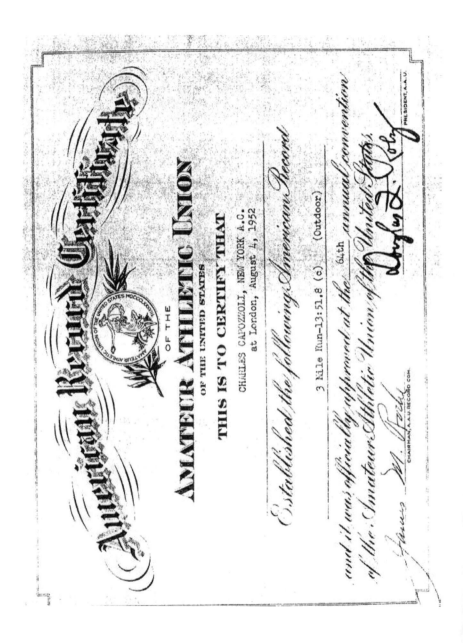

Chapter 12
"Senior Year at Georgetown"

After arriving home in New York from England, the Olympic Games now being over, I spent several weeks with my parents before returning to Georgetown, only to be interrupted by a trip to Toronto, Canada. I had been invited to run in the Canadian National Exhibition track events, the ten mile run and the three-mile run.

Finally, I was to run the longest distance race of my career. Since the airlines were on strike, I had to take a train from New York to Toronto. It was a long trip, sitting up all night, getting very little sleep. The train arrived about 8:00am. The ten-mile race was to start at 9:00am. I took a cab to the stadium. When I arrived, the race was ready to begin without me.

The starter of the race saw me waving to him, held up the race, and said to me, "I can hold the race up to give you time to change into your track gear, but you won't be able to warm up."

Warm up! I've been up all night on the train and was ready for bed, no less a ten mile run. Can you imagine this? In the center of the track, a "circus" was going on, trapeze stunts, elephants, etc. What did I get myself into?

The gun went off! Oh! Only ten miles to go before I could go to the hotel and to bed. One half of the track was pavement, the other cinders. I wore my out-door spike shoes.

With three miles to go, a friend yells, "go now, Charlie!"

Was he kidding? Three more miles to go and he's telling me to put on the steam. I wanted to quit and grab a cab back to the hotel. I won the race in record time, per the article that follows. I went back to the hotel, rested up for the next day's event, the three-mile run. When I woke up that morning, I could hardly walk. My muscles tightened up like never before. Off to the stadium I went. I'm now on the start of the three-mile run. At least this race was two thirds less than the day before. I won, but never went back to Canada again.

Remember? These were the days of amateur track. We didn't get paid to run. We did it for the glory of the sport and loved it. Our joy was the sport of it, the friendships made, and the thrill of competing. (But no more three ring circus, unless they wanted another clown!)

The few weeks with mom and dad went by fast. It's now my senior year at Georgetown. I was honored for my achievements in making the Olympic Team and setting an American three-mile run record in England. I had a new roommate, Al Triandafilou, who to this day is one of my closest friends, more like a brother. Unlike my Canadian roommate, Don Stonehouse, when I was a freshman, I was better able to understand Al who was from Boston. He and I were the most popular guys on campus. Our room smelled like an Italian Greek grocery market. Al's parents sent him delicious Greek pastries. Mom and dad sent me salami and sharp Italian provolone cheese. The smell permeated throughout the corridor. We shared our goodies with the other students. The smell attracted them to our room.

Cross-country season now began, running against Annapolis, Maryland University, and several others in Virginia. The big race was the IC4A Five Mile Run at Van Cortland Park in New York where I had run in high school (got lost twice). This was it! Get lost in this one and you're in deep trouble. Frank Sevigne will shoot you. The gun went off (not Sevigne's). There were hundreds of contestants running to get to the narrow pathway leading into the hills. By the time you got to this point, you were already exhausted. One stretch up a hill was called, "cemetery hill!" We knew why. I took the lead only when I was sure of not getting lost or running into a chain link fence as I did in that race in Virginia. With several hundred yards to go, I picked up the pace, winning in record time. This made the front pages of the New York News and the Mirror, two of the most widely read papers, in addition to the New York Times. While it was a great thrill for me, it was even greater for my parents, especially dad who read these newspapers everyday.

Our team returned to Georgetown to continue training and studies. The following week, after the IC4A's, Frank Sevigne, our coach, sent me alone to Michigan to run in the NCAA 4 Mile Cross Country Run. Never ran there so I stayed with the pack until I knew I was coming into the home stretch. I won and set a new NCAA record. One of the articles read, "Spaghetti eater wins!"

Late that night, I boarded a plane back to Washington D.C. As the plane descended to land, about mid-night, the captain announced, "Will Charlie Capozzoli please be the last one to disembark the plane!"

What did I do now? I just wanted to get a cab to Georgetown and go to bed. As I exited from the plane, the Georgetown band was playing alma mater songs, students were cheering, hundreds of them. They put me on their shoulders, carried me to the main terminal where they lifted Frank Sevigne (my coach) onto their shoulders. They were a happy group of students, but not as happy as they made me. There was then a car caravan back to the university. How could anyone sleep after this?

The next day an article read, "Capozzoli is greeted by cheering students, outdoing the victorious Maryland football team." It was also announced on the radio.

"Do your best, my son, Run to Win. It's love that really matters!"

in NCAA Meet

* * *

Lone Entry

Charley Capozzoli

Team Title for State

Record Is Set by Capozzoli

By PAUL CHANDLER

EAST LANSING, Mich., Nov. 25.—Despite a lifetime spaghetti diet the nation's finest cross-country runner weighs only 125 pounds.

Charley Capozzoli, son of a Flushing, N. Y., shoemaker, won the annual four-mile NCAA gallop here Monday, while Michigan State took the team championship to give the Spartans a unique sweep of the "triple crown" of cross-country in this area. Coach Karl Schlademan's squad earlier had won the Big Ten and IC4A titles.

Capozzoli didn't have a chance to join a team victory because he was the only entry from Georgetown University.

When he goes home, mama and papa stuff him with spaghetti and meat balls. He doesn't get much of that at school. But after he won the IC4A title a fortnight ago, the prize at his home was a huge Italian dinner.

Twenty-one years old and 5 feet 8, Capozzoli has an extraordinarily long stride, which has been trying to chop to his size. Running in almost perfect weather conditions over firm turf, he won Monday's race by 120 yards over Ray Osterhout, of Syracuse.

His winning time of 19:36.7 was a course and NCAA record since all NCAA meets have been held over the Michigan State course. Bob Black of Penn State in 1950 set the old record of 19:52.33.

Schlademan called the winner "the greatest undergraduate distance runner the U. S. ever has produced." Capozzoli's best time for a mile is 4:13.6 and his best for two miles, 9:04.0, both being clocked in European exhibitions.

Capozzoli Cops 10-Mile Race In Record Time

TORONTO, Aug. 30 (*P*)—Rev. Bob Richards of Laverne, Calif., United States Olympic pole vault champion and record holder, smashed two of his own Canadian records at the Canadian National exhibition track meet.

With a vault of 15 feet ¼ inches, he smashed the meet record of 14 feet 7¾ inches he set here last year and the Canadian Open mark of 14 feet 10¼ inches he made in Toronto in 1950.

Another U. S. Olympic team member, Wes Santee of the University of Kansas, won the 880-yard and one-mile handicaps. His time of 1:58.6 in the 880 event broke the meet record set by Geoff Dooley of Montreal last year. The time for the mile was 4:25.

* * *

JIM GATHERS, member of the United States Air Force stationed at Geneva, N. Y., and Olympic athlete, failed to qualify in the 100-yard dash but won the 220-yard event in :21.2.

Flushing's Charles Capozzoli of Georgetown set a meet record of 55 minutes 24 seconds in winning the 10-mile race.

The Washington Melrose Club won the team title with 28 points. The Ledroit Park Falcons of Washington were second with 21.

Charlie Capozzoli, slim Bayside high school lad, who sped to a new clocking in winning the NCAA cross country championship on top of winning the IC4A harrier crown, got the royal reception he rated when he returned to Georgetown University after the meet . . . he was met at the Washington station by the school band and a roaring throng of students who formed an autocade with blaring horns to let folks know they were welcoming a true national champion . . . Charlie, as fine a young man as you'll ever meet in sports, rates all the glory and attention he's getting . . . he wears the mantle of a champion with quiet dignity and grace.

Daily Mirror

Vol. 29. No. 127.   NEW YORK 17, N. Y., TUESDAY, NOVEMBER 18, 1952

GOOD TURN. Competitors in the IC4A 5-mile Cross Country at Van Cortland Park round the first turn after start of race. Winner was Charles Capozzoli, of Georgetown, who ran the course in 24 minutes, 30.1 seconds.

(Mirror Photos by Anthony Remate)
FIRST FIVE in the IC4A race line up after the finish, L. to r.: Charles Capozzoli, Georgetown, first; Ray Osterhout, Syracuse, second; James R. Kepford, Michigan State, third; John Barry, Villanova, fourth, and Fred Dwyer, Villanova, fifth. Michigan State took the team title with a low of 46 points.

N.Y.U.'s George King crosses finish line first to capture IC4A freshman race over the three-mile course at Van Cortlandt Park yesterday.
(Mirror Photo)

Capozzoli IC4A X-Country King

Charlie Capozzoli, a slim Georgetown senior who learned plenty as a member of the U. S. Olympic team last Summer, won the individual championship of the IC4A cross country run at Van Cortlandt Park yesterday, but Michigan State carried off the team title.

The 21-year-old Capozzoli, who wears sneakers instead of spikes, went around the five-mile course in a phenomenal 24.30.1, which shaved just 25 seconds off Dick Shea's winning time of last year —and that was the fastest in history of meet.

The course was altered somewhat this year, and in the process officials smoothed out some of the rough spots and eliminated some of the running through the woods. That accounted for the speedy clocking.

Michigan State won it easily taking third, seventh, eighth, ninth and 19th for 46 points. Army, the Heptagonal winner last week, was second with 92, followed by Syracuse with 98, defending champion Penn State with 109 and Georgetown with...

SPORTS   THE NEW YORK TIMES, TUESDAY, NOVEMBER 18, 1952.

Capozzoli Triumphs Impressively in I. C. 4-A Cr

GEORGETOWN STAR WINNER IN 24:30.1

Hill-and-Dalers in Their Five-Mile Run at Van Cortlandt Park

Capozzoli Scores Easily Over Syracuse's Osterhout With Brilliant 5-Mile Time

MICHIGAN STATE ON TOP

Dominates the I. C. 4-A. Team Contest—Freshman Run Is Taken by King, N. Y. U.

By JOSEPH M. SHEEHAN

With one of the most impressive performances in the forty-four-year history of the event, Charley Capozzoli of Georgetown yesterday scored a runaway victory in the Intercollegiate A. A. A. varsity cross-country championship. Michigan State's solid squad quietly outclassed its Eastern competition in the battle for team honors.

Taking charge after the first mile, Capozzoli poured on the pace steadily to come bounding some 150 yards in front of his nearest rival in a 169-runner field. The ardent 24-year-old Hoya sensation covered the Van Cortlandt Park course's five miles of hill and dale in the remarkable time of 24 minutes 30.1 seconds.

Cross-country courses vary too much for serious attention to be paid to records, but it is doubtful any certified five-mile harrier route has been traveled faster in this country. The best previous clocking for the distance in Van Cortlandt Park, over a slightly different route, was 24:35.1, Jimmy Dixie Shea posted that a year ago in the last of his three successive I. C. 4-A. victories.

Caps Steady Development

Capozzoli's brilliant performance capped three years of steady development under the coaching of Hank Sevigne. The 5 feet 8 inch, 130-pound Flushing youth, a local schoolboy mile and cross-country champion at Bryant High, captured the I. C. 4-A. two-mile title last spring, made the Olympic team as a 5,000-meter man and, in the post-Olympic United States-British Empire meet won the three-mile event in 13:51.8, the fastest time recorded for that distance outdoors by an American.

Favored yesterday off this background, Capozzoli added to his stature as an American international distance-running hopeful with a race that left observing coaches, as well as his rivals, gasping.

Ray Osterhout, the Syracuse ace who beat Charley for the runner-up prize last year, hung closely to Capozzoli's heels through the first tour of the hills and had to let him go on the long swing around the flats. By the three-mile pole, which he passed in 14:36, Georgetown's winner was fifteen yards inf ront, going away with every stride.

Giving up his vain pursuit, Osterhout concentrated on holding second place and did so, by some fifteen yards, against the strong bid of Michigan State's Jim Kepford, runners-up in last Friday's Big Ten championship. Kepford passed John Joe Barry, Villanova's Irish-trained star, on Cemetery Hill, at the start of the

The varsity runners crossing a bridge during the I. C. 4-A. event

The first five in the order in which they finished, left to right: Charles Capozzoli of Georgetown, Raymond L. Osterhout of Syracuse, James R. Kepford of Michigan State, John Barry of Villanova and Fred Dwyer of Villanova.

2 VICTORIES GAINED BY MISS HEEMSKERK

Fannie Heemskerk of the Netherlands, her condition much improved.

teenth. The triumphs advanced Miss Heemskerk to fourth place in the standing.

Miss Heemskerk's ninth-round game with Valentina Belova, second in the standing, remains un-

who defeated Josna Langos of Hungary.

STANDING OF THE PLAYERS

SETS CROSS-COUNTRY RECORD: Charlie Capozzoli, left, of Georgetown, whose time of 1 minutes 36.7 seconds over the four-mile course at Michigan State yesterday bettered tl N. C. A. A. mark of 19:52.3, held since 1948 by Bob Black of Rhode Island State. With Capozzl are Ray Osterhout of Syracuse, second, and Jim Kepford of Michigan State, third.

Free Press Photo by Bud Johnson
VICTOR DASHES TO PHONE
Call to coach comes first

Georgetown Ace Wins NCAA Crown

NCAA HARRIER MARK BROKEN BY CAPOZZOLI

Hoya Star Captures Event in 19:36.7

East Lansing, Mich., Nov. 24 (AP)—Charlie Capozzoli, a 125-pound featherweight runner from Georgetown university, whizzed around the four mile course in a winning time of 19 minutes, 36.7 seconds to set a new N.C.A.A. cross-country record here today.

His time shattered the old record of 19:52.3 set by Bob Boack, "the Flying Skeleton" of Rhode Island State, in 1948.

Michigan State won the team title with a low of 65 points, barely edging out second-place Indiana with 68 points. The victory made Michigan State the undisputed national cross-country champ since the Spartans previously had taken firsts in the Big Ten and IC4A meets.

Iowa was third with 103 points and Syracuse and Penn State tied for fourth with 110 points each.

Comes From Behind

Capozzoli, a one-man entry, came here without a coach, trainer or companion. He was the IC4A individual winner and was a U. S. Olympic team member in the 5,000 meter run.

A dark-haired, slender youth of Italian descent, Capozzoli is 21 and a senior at Georgetown. His father operates a shoe repair business at Flushing, N. Y.

Dick Ferguson of Iowa was in the lead at the one mile mark but Capozzoli overtook him halfway around the course and was in front of the pack of 97 runners the rest of the way.

He was clocked at 9:50.5 at the two mile mark and 14:46.0 at the three mile point. He breezed home still going strong 100 yards ahead of second-place Ray Osterhout of Syracuse at the finish.

"I felt I was going good all the way around." Capozzoli said. "I really pushed myself those last two miles but I had no idea I was going to set a record."

Spaghetti-Eater

The Winner

Grand Slam For State

M. S. C. Harriers Take NCAA Title to Complete Sweep of Titles

Michigan State's cross-country team grand-slammed the field to win a clean-cut title to the national title today. The Spartans won the National Collegiate Athletic association championship at noon to go along with their previously earned Big Ten and eastern titles, a triple crown.

Paced by Capt. Jim Kepford of Muskegon the Spartans edged Indiana in a 13-team race over the four-mile course at the college. State finished with a team total of 65 points, three less than the Hoosiers with 68.

Winning its third title of the season, the Spartans' team effort

The WASHINGTON DAILY News

32d Year—No. 15 · *Dl. 7777* · *Entered as Second-Class Matter at D. C. Post Office*

CITY EDITION **TUESDAY, NOVEMBER 25, 1952**

Index

Classified ..48-53
Columnists ...27
Donnelly 32
Editorial 26
Night Clubs...35
Pictures ...28-29
Radio-TV ..54-55
Sports . 41-47
Theaters ...32-34
Women's ...36-38
Your Health ..33

Charlie Capozzoli, at left aloft, was met by 500 cheering Georgetown University students at National Airport early today on his return from the National Collegiate Athletic Association's cross country championship race—which he won. Charlie went alone to East Lansing, Mich., and ran the four-mile grind in 19 minutes, 36.7 seconds yesterday, breaking a record that has stood since 1936. That's his coach, Frank Sevigne, shaking his hand, right. (Story on Page 46.) News Staff Photo by Lawrence Krebs

111

s Herald Sports

For tops
Follow Padd
Herald. Reco
the nation's
cappers, Pad
picked the

TUESDAY, NOVEMBER 25, 1952

Telephone, REpublic 1234

Loyal Hoya Students Go Wild Over Charlie

[Times-Herald Staff Photo]

Charlie Capozzoli, 1952 Olympic runner, gets a free ride from some of the welcome body of Hoya students who turned out at the National airport last night to greet the Georgetown university star on his victorious return from Lansing, Mich., where he set a new N.C.A.A. record for the four-mile cross-country run. His time was 19:36.7. His record time shattered the old mark of 19:52.3 set in 1948.

CHARLIE, THEIR BOY—Charlie Capozzoli of Georgetown University receives a champion's welcome at the National Airport on his arrival home from Lansing, Mich., where he won the NCAA cross country title in record time of 19:36.7.

A car caravan of 400 students and the band met the 21-year-old senior. Above, he and Coach Frank Sevigne are hoisted to shoulders of the students. Capozzoli was a member of the United States Olympic team.

Capozzoli Gets Hero's Welcome

Early this morning Charlie Capozzoli had his second breathless moment. When 500 wildly cheering classmates from Georgetown University swept him off a Capital Airliner at National Airport, hoisted his 125-pounds to their collective shoulders and paraded him thru the massive administration buildin, Charlie was all smiles and out of breath.

A few hours earlier the Hoya harrier gasped for air as he crossed the finish line of the NCAA cross country championship race 30 yards ahead of the field to set a new record of 19:36.7 voer the four mile course at Michigan State University.

It was evident upon his arrival here he didn't expect the overwhelming reception he got. The Georgetown University band marched up and down the ramp a few times and when Charlie alighted from the huge airliner it swung into a thumping march. This immediately was drowned out by the thunderous cheers of those 500 students as they carted the amazed runner upstairs.

UNEXPECTED

There he managed to thank the boys and choke out, "Gosh, I never

expected anything like this." Track and field Coach Frank Sevigne then was carried over and the two shook hands.

The good looking youngster has been a one-man publicity agent for Georgetown. Just a week ago the 21-year-old native of Garden City, Long Island captured the IC4A title in New York. Last summer he went to the Olympics.

For yesterday's competition the school didn't bother to send a team up to Michigan. It sent Charlie and that was enough. He's the only long distance runner the school can claim altho Carl Joyce and Tom Voorhees are a pair of outstanding two-mile relay runners.

Coach Sevigne is responsible for

discovering the speedy, durable lightweight. Sevigne came to Georgetown in the fall of 1949 from Seton Hall in New Jersey and brought Capozzoli, Joyce and Voorhees with him. But for winning national long distance running honors it's like one of the boys shouted in the lobby this morning when Sevigne tried to express his thanks to the students for turning out, "the thanks belong to Charlie."

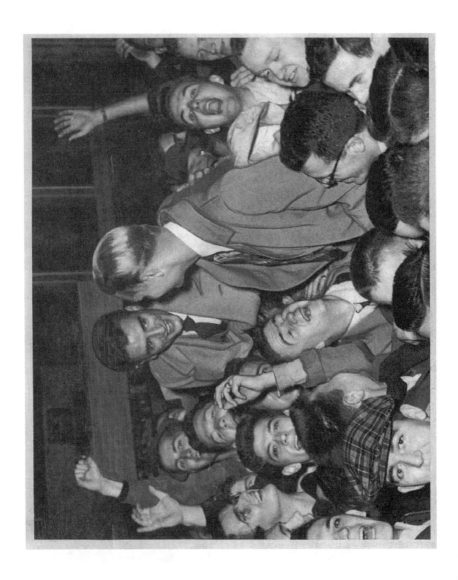

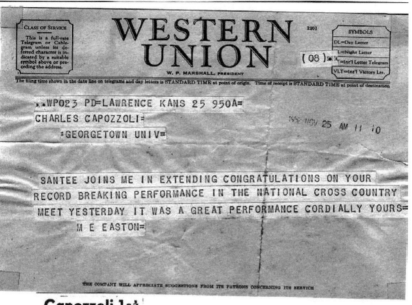

x▪WP023 PD=LAWRENCE KANS 25 950A=

CHARLES CAPOZZOLI=

=GEORGETOWN UNIV=

SANTEE JOINS ME IN EXTENDING CONGRATULATIONS ON YOUR
RECORD BREAKING PERFORMANCE IN THE NATIONAL CROSS COUNTRY
MEET YESTERDAY IT WAS A GREAT PERFORMANCE CORDIALLY YOURS=

M E EASTON=

Capozzoli 1st In NCAA Run, Clips Record

EAST LANSING, Mich., Nov. 24 (UP). Charles Capozzoli, of Georgetown University, won the N.C.A.A. cross country championship race today in the record time of 19:36.7.

Capozzoli, the favorite who a week ago captured the IC4A title in New oYrk, finished first by 30 yards. He took the lead after the big pack of runners passed the mile mark and led the rest of the race over Michigan State's four-mile hill and dale course.

Capozzoli's time smashed the old record of 19:52.3 set in 1948 by Robert Black of Rhode Island State. Ray Osterhout, of Syracuse, finished second while Michigan State's Jim Kepford was third. Fourth place went to Jack Wellman, of Indiana University.

Michigan State captured the team title. The Spartan harriers scored 65 points to nose out second place Indiana which finished with 68.

Syracuse, defending team champions, tied with Penn State for third place with 110 points each while Miami (Ohio) was fifth with 145 points and San Diego State sixth with 181.

Mark Man. Charlie Capozzoli (left) of Georgetown is congratulated by runnersup Ray Osterhout (center) of Syracuse and Michigan State's Jim Kepford. Charlie had just set NCAA cross-country mark in Lansing, Mich. *-Story on page 62*

"Perry Como, Frank Sinatra,
And Tony Bennett"

As mentioned previously, I met Perry Como when I was twelve years old at his birthday party given by his fan club. Six years later, the night after graduation from high school, my good friends and teammates went to a small night club where Tony Bennett entertained us most of the evening. I then met Frank Sinatra three years later in the lobby of the Ambassador Hotel, in Los Angeles, and attended his "opening night" at the "Cocoanut Grove" as his guest along with my team-mates. Amazing, huh? I use to listen to them on the radio, "battle of the baritones," every Sunday at home when fourteen years old and dreamt of being a singer like them. I bought all of their records, played them over and over again, singing along with them, and later in life got to meet them. "Como, Capozzoli, Remigino!" Well, I never saw Perry Como again, but in 1952, the Unico National Awards for "Outstanding Italian American men and women for 1951" was "Perry Como, singer," "Charles Capozzoli and Lindy Remigino, Track and Field!" I didn't attend the award ceremonies for some reason, but wished that I did. It would have been nice to see Perry Como once again.

Did I ever get to sing? My college teammates, Ed Kirk, Vince Kelly, and myself, did lots of singing at Georgetown, in the showers, in the hallways (dorms), and when traveling in the car to and from track meets. Vince Kelly, our teammate, a good friend to this day, outdid us with his beautiful tenor voice. He still sings at various functions. We get together from time to time, but no longer sing as a "shower trio." It's surprising that the Jesuits at Georgetown didn't stop us from our loud singing that echoed from the showers throughout the dorms. We really belted out songs like, "Anytime—O My Papa—Volare—and—Twas Just A Garden In The Rain."

When attending a college dance at the Shoreham Hotel in Washington D.C., my senior year, I finally got up the nerve to go on the stage, grab a microphone, and sing a few lines, "You Belong To Me." Guess I did pretty well, since everyone kept on dancing and I wasn't thrown off the stage. Dad would have been proud of me?

116

That was the beginning and end of my singing career. Dad was right! "Stick to running, my son."

"Dream, my son, dream of wondrous things."
"It's love that really matters!"

UNICO NATIONAL
"Headin' for Columbus, The Buckeye Capital"

Subject: Unico National Convention

Hotel: Deshler-Wallick Hotel

Refreshments: Smorgasbord (Anything and everything good to eat)

Program and Highlights: Ladies Reception Governors Mansion

Memorial to Don Gentile

Dates: August 20-24th, 1952

Entertainment: Golf tournament, swimming, bocci, card games, shuffleboard, pool tables, playgrounds for children, dancing, singing, picnic De Luxe, 4 days of Dream Vacation with fun, laughter and sports.

Speakers: Georgia Neese Clark
Mayor James Rhodes

Awards to the following Outstanding Italian-American Men and Women for Year 1951:

Perry Como, Singer, Radio City, New York; William C. Davini, Assistant Superintendent of schools, St. Paul, Minn.; Hon. Michael V. DiSalle, Former Mayor of Toledo and former Director of Price Stabilization; Jimmy Durante, Comedian, Hollywood, California; Hon. Vincent R. Impelliteri, Mayor of New York City; Mario Lanza, Singer, Hollywood, California; Rt. Rev. Msgr. Luigi Ligutti, Leader in Rural Education, Des Moines, Iowa; Mrs. Francesca Brogiotti Lodge, wife of John Davis Lodge, Governor of Connecticut; Judge Juvenal Marchisio, Boys Town of Italy, New York City; Ezio Pinza, Opera Star, Television, Movies, Radio, Hollywood, California; Hon. John O. Pastore, Senator from Rhode Island.

Award to the Outstanding Italian-American Athletes for the year 1951-52:

Bengal Boxing	**Soccer Player**
Dominic Napolitano—Notre Dame	Charley Colombo—St. Louis
Champion Billiard	**College Football Coach**
Willie Mosconi—Haverton, Pa.	Art Raimo—Villanova
Track	**Pro Football Coach**
Charles Capozzoli—Georgetown	Gene Ronzani—Green Bay Packers
Lindy Remigino—Manhattan	**College Basketball Coach**
Rookie Players	Bob Vanotta—Southwest Teachers College,
Ralph Guglielmi—Notre Dame	Springfield, Missouri
Alan Ameche—Wisconsin	**Pro Basketball Coach**
Wrestling	Al Cervi—Syracuse National
Frank Bettucci—Cornell University	**College Basketball Player**
Pro Baseball Players	Bob Sassone—St. Bonaventure
Vic Raschi—New York Yanks, American League	**Pro Golf**
Sal Maglie—New York Giants, National League	John Revolta—Evanston, Illinois
Pitcher	**Amateur Golf**
Ed Cereghino—Kansas City Blues	Frank Strafaci—Flushing, Long Island
Umpire	Louis Montaleone—Kansas City, Missouri
"Babe" Pinelli—National League	

Dr. D. M. Nigro Award

Henry "Hank" Lauricella—Tennessee—Most Valuable Italian-American Athlete of the Year—1951-52

Former Winners of the Most Valuable Athlete of the Year: Charlie Trippi, Angelo Bertelli, Alex Scarpico, Arnold Galiffa, Anthony Minisi, John Panelli, Archie Sam Romoni, Paul Governali, Tony Cemore, Sam Urgetta and Harry Stella.

Awards to the Outstanding Italians of Kansas City.

Chapter 13
"Capozzoli, Ashenfelter,
And Cosgul, The Turk"

After a successful cross country season, indoor track began in January. I won the two-mile run in the Washington Star games. The time was slow, but I won, "Run to Win!"

In a week or two, the big meet, the Knights of Columbus, took place in Boston. The favorite to win the two mile run was Horace Ashenfelter, the Olympic Steeplechase Champion, who set an Olympic record in Helsinki. Cosgul, the Turk, from Turkey, another Olympian, was considered second choice. I was the sleeper in the race. Having changed my running stride after returning from Europe, practicing hard like the great European runners, and having more confidence, I planned my race. Rather than taking the lead as I did in the 5,000 meter heat in Helsinki, I planned to stay behind Ashenfelter and Cosgul as I did in the race against Pirie in England. Ashenfelter took the lead as expected, with Cosgul close behind, and I got farther behind than planned. Ashenfelter set a fast pace. I said to myself, "Do your best!"

As far as everyone was concerned, I might end up taking third place. With six laps to go (22 laps for two-miles indoors) I felt good. Gradually I gained ground, but not enough to be noticed by the crowd or Ashenfelter. With four laps to go, the gap was narrowing! The crowd now perked up and sensed something was happening.

I passed Ashenfelter with a burst of speed (those Angels) with three laps to go. The crowd now began to roar. It sounded like a tornado in the making. I lapped Cosgul, the Turk, and crossed the finish line 60 yards ahead of Ashenfelter. As I crossed the finish line, the lights dimmed in the garden and a spotlight followed me around the track. (Was this getting me ready for the circus in Canada, ha-ha!).

It was announced that I had run the fastest collegiate two mile in history, 8:55.2. I was voted the outstanding performer, receiving the majority of votes. The meet promoters approached me, congratulating me for such a great performance. They asked if I would meet them in their office stating that I deserved something more than a trophy. My guess was that it was money. I asked if they would please put it in the poor box of the nearest Catholic Church. Being the "Knights of Columbus" track meet, I could think of no objections to my request.

THE CHRISTIAN SCIENCE MONITOR, BOSTON, MONDAY.

Boston Indoor Meet Winners

CHARLES CAPAZZOLI OF GEORGETOWN UNIV. WON THE LEO LARRIVEE TWO MILE RUN IN 8:55.3. IT WAS THE FASTEST TWO MILE RUN BY A COLLEGIAN. CAPAZZOLI WAS VOTED THE OUTSTANDING PERFORMER OF THE MEET.

VETERAN DISTANCE RUNNER FRED WILT GOT OFF TO A HEAD START IN HIS ANNUAL MILE RIVALRY WITH DON GEHRMANN BY WINNING THE KC MILE IN 4:10.5.

OLYMPIC CHAMPION REV. BOB RICHARDS CONTINUES AS THE PREMIER POLE VAULTER IN THE WORLD. HE CLEARED 15'3" AT THE MEET.

"Run to Win! Never give up! Dream of wondrous things! Nothing is impossible! It's love that really matters!"

CAPOZZOLI TRIUMPHS IN K.C. 2-MILE UPSET

Hoya Ace Sets Record of 8:55.3

Wilt 4:10.5 Mile Victor; Marks Go in Jumps, 1000

By WILL CLONEY

Charlie Capozzoli, a tiny Georgetown senior with a pair of pistons for legs, stole the hearts of 12,151 spectators in the Garden last night when he whipped Olympic Horace Ashenfelter in the fastest two-mile performance ever recorded by a collegian.

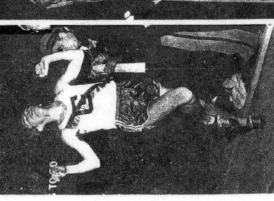

SOME OF THE THRILLS at the K. of C. track meet in the Leo Larrivee two-mile run in 8:55.3 for a new meet record. At left, Chuck Capozzoli of Georgetown snaps tape to win the to place second behind Bob Richards. At right, Don Laz clears pin bar in the pole vault

Fastest College 2-Mile in History; rth Carolina, G.W. Loses at State

Hoya Upsets Ashenfelter By 45 Yards In 8:55.3

BOSTON SUNDAY POST, JANUARY 18, 1953

CAPOZZOLI BREAKS K. OF C. TWO-MILE RECORD

BOSTON, Jan. 17—Georgetown University's 136-pound Charlie Capozzoli ran the fastest two-mile race ever turned in by a collegian And up set the famed Horace Ashenfelter in the Boston Knights of Columbus Meet here tonight.

The Hoya senior from Flushing, Long Island, was timed in 8:55.3, breaking the meet record of 9:00.4 set by Greg Rice 12 years ago. It was the first time Capozzoli has been clocked under the nine-minute mark and it compared favorably with the American indoor record of 8:50.7, held by Fred Wilt.

Capozzoli, the NCAA and ICAA cross country champion, paced himself beautifully. He chased Ashenfelter. America's record breaking Olympic steeplechase champion through a 4:28.6 mile from a 20-yard distance.

Wins by 45 Yards

Four hundred yards from the finish, Cappy began a mad sprint that caught Ashenfelter, and as the surprised crowd roared its approval. Capozzoli steamed home the victor by 45 yards. The Georgetown star was never worse than third. Olympic steeplechaser Browning Ross wound up third and Turkish Olympian Osman Coskul was fourth.

Capozzoli was one of three Georgetowners in the meet, and the other two, Joe LaPierre, in the mile, and Carl Joyce, in the 1000-yard run, won a third and second place, respectively.

LaPierre ran a 4:11.3 mile, but finished 7 yards behind the winner, Fred Wilt of New York A. C. Second, a stride ahead of LaPierre was Sweden's Ingvar Ericsson. LaPierre had the distinction of beating out last year's king of the milers. Don Gehrmann, who wound up fourth.

Defender Fred Dwyer of Villanova set a meet record of 2:11.6 while racing to a 5 yard triumph over Joyce in the 1000. The old mark of 2:11.9 was set by Campbell Kane of Indiana University in 1941.

Capozzoli Voted K. C. Meet's Best; Great Duels Loom With Ashenfelter

Capozzoli New Track Darling

Capozzoli Voted K. C. Meet's Best; Great Duels Loom With Ashenfelter

By BOB HOLBROOK

Salient facts emanating from the K. of C. meet were:

1—Fred Wilt may quit track shortly.

2—Ingvar Ericsson, Swedish mile champion, is one of the finest to visit here and may wipe a record off the boards before he leaves for Stockholm Feb. 15.

3—Charley Capozzoli, diminutive Georgetown two-miler, could be the first American to break 8:50 in the two-mile.

4—Mal Whitfield, Olympic 800 meter champ, will set a new 600-yard record this season.

5—Local track officials need extra practice in arranging the cross bars on both the pole vault and high jump for record-trying performances.

Ericsson Impresses

Wilt won a 4:10.5 mile over Ericsson while suffering the effects of a virus infection. He's finding it increasingly difficult to maintain top condition at 32 and since he already holds the world's indoor two-mile record he'll probably hang up his spikes within the next month.

Ericsson created considerable of a stir as second place finisher in the mile. It was apparent to all and sundry that here is a miler of exceptional talent. In his first try on the boards he whizzed to a 4:11.2 effort and could have won the race handily except for inexperience on the turns.

The outstanding performer of the night, however, was Capozzoli, 22-year-old Queens product. "I never thought I was ready for that," he said after turning in an 8:55.5 two mile victory over Horace Ashenfelter.

It was the fastest two-mile Capozzoli ever ran and the fastest ever by an American collegian. Last week, for instance, he ran the two miles at Washington in 9:17.

Easily the Standout

Running Ashenfelter into the boards (he beat him by a quarter of a lap) is quite an accomplishment, Capozzoli left the large crowd limp with his tremendous surge and he likened this race to one last Summer when he ran the fastest three miles ever credited to an American. It was in England in a race against Britain's Pirie.

Unfortunately, there was no trophy for the meet's outstanding performer. Had there been, Cappy would have won it. Anyway, the sportswriters took a poll and he won the vote hands down. For lack once there was no question who was top performer.

Ashenfelter was stunned when Cappy turned on the heat and kept on going

"He deserved it," remarked the F.B.I. agent, "He has worked hard."

HELLO, MOM—Charley Capozzoli, Georgetown runner, calls his mother after racing fastest two-mile ever by a collegian.

Ashenfelter worked hard, too. "Maybe too hard," he said.

"But we'll see what happens next week," he warned.

If Ashenfelter and Capozzoli engage in a friendly feud this indoor season—and it begins to shape up that way—there's no telling what will happen to the two-mile mark.

Experts feel that Capozzoli will develop into one of the greatest runners in our history.

"If he can run 8:55.5 now," asked one track follower, "what's he going to be doing a month from now?"

Whitfield in Shape

Mal Whitfield is in better shape now for the indoor season since he's been discharged from the Air Force. He has more time to train and his 1:12 for the 600 was flossy enough.

But George Rhoden, also an Olympic champion, was disappointed in Whitfield's time.

He told Mal that he would have stepped up the pace for the first quarter had he realized it was so slow.

Rhoden told Whitfield:

"You could have done 1:10." A time of 1:10.0 would knock two tenths of a second off Johnny Borican's and Hugh Short's indoor record.

The record attempts in the high jump and pole vault stymied the officials. They had difficulty raising the cross bar for Richards' pole vault at 15 ft. 6 in. They had more trouble measuring the high jump cross bar at 6 ft. 9 in., for a new world record try by Art Wiesner and Arnold Betton. (They failed).

They'll be more accustomed to it at the B. A. A. meet two weeks hence.

Hollis Triumphs in Physique Contest

Bob Hollis of Troy, N. Y., a freshman at Springfield College, won the Mr. Boston physique contest of 1953 at the Boston Y. M. C. U. last night.

Hollis, who took the Mr. Eastern Massachusetts title last Nov. 23, represented the Springfield College Barbell Club in a preliminary weight-lifting contest and won easily in the light-heavy class.

Harry Vieweg, Lawrence, placed second in the physique contest, and Alfred Poulin, Manchester, N. H., was third.

Weight-lifting results:

123-pounds—Won by Paul Dussault, Woonsocket, R. I.; 2. Paul DeJesus, Pawtucket, R. I.; 3. Herbert J. Muse, Wakefield.

132-pounds—Won by Edward O. Goyette, Dedham; 2. Paul Hartford, Wakefield.

148-pounds—Won by Roland Thibeault, Woonsocket, R. I.; 2. Bert St. George, Boston.

165-pounds—Won by Arthur Butz, Long Island, N. Y.; 2. Andrew Achondy, Haverhill; 3. Armand LaMarr, Holyoke.

181-pounds—Won by Robert Hollis, Troy, N. Y.; 2. Francis Lucia, Haverhill; 3. Ray A. Bialecki, Worcester.

198-pounds—Won by Raymond Racine, Woonsocket, R. I.; 2. Robert Dupre, Woonsocket, R. I.; 3. Arthur Dandereau.

Heavyweight—Won by Elisha Grant, Woburn; 2. Bill Look, Haverhill.

Catholic League

MISSION (42)	G	F	P		LAWRENCE CENTRAL (21)	G	F	P
McDonald rf	2	1	5		Flynn lg	1	0	2
McAdams lf	4	1	13		Collins lg	0	2	2
Power c	6	1	13		Tre chaud rg	3	2	8
Galvin rg	3	0	6		Noble rg	2	4	8
Kenneally lg	1	0	2		McCafferty c	0	1	1
Clark lg	0	0	0		Graves lf	1	0	2
					Fiorino rf	3	0	6
Totals	18	6	42		Totals	12	13	37

At Danvers

ST. JOHN'S (52)	G	F	P		ST. MARY'S (47)	G	F	P
Pigott rf	3	2	8		Burke lg	4	0	8
Donnelly lf	2	2	6		Dunn rg	2	1	5
McCarthy c	7	3	17		Ayotte rg	0	0	0
Fahey rg	6	0	12		Smyzynski c	3	0	6
Donnelly rg	0	0	0		McLaghlin lf	2	1	5
Wk'nh's't lg	3	0	7		Lynch rf	7	3	17
Graczyk lg	1	0	1		Tibbets rf	2	0	4
Totals	21	10	52		Totals	17	13	47

At Jamaica Plain

IMMACULATE CONCEPTION (New.) (77)	G	F	P		ST. THOMAS (39)	G	F	P
Coter rf	4	0	8		Cullen lg			
Finnegan rf	0	0	0		Barrett lg			
Manning lf	10	2	22		Harrinet'n rg			
Twomey lf	1	1	3		Costello rf			
Foley c	11	3	25		Keane lf			
O'Brien lg	4	5	13		Harmon rf			
Donovan rg	1	1	3		Totals	16	7	39
Roche lg	2	1	5					
Cashman lg	0	0	0					
Totals	33	11	77					

At Somerville

ST. CLEMENT'S (57)	G	F	P		IMMACULATE (46)	G	F	P
Whalen rf	7	0	14		Redington lg			
Cirame lf	7	0	14		O'Hara rg			
Casper lf	1	0	2		Boyle c			

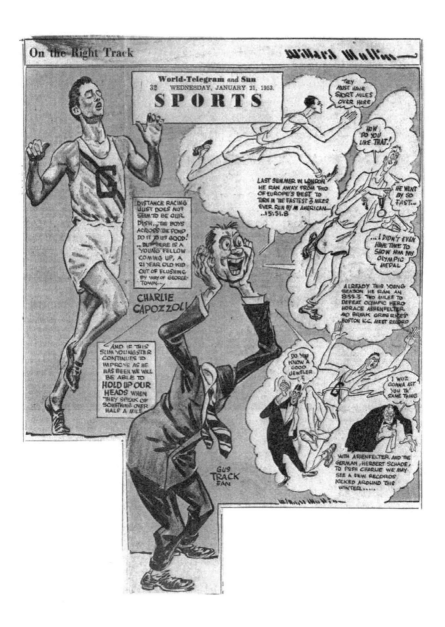

"I Lapped The Turk"
Shouts Capozzoli

BY WILL CLONEY

Boston Post Sports Editor

It was getting late on that January night in 1953, and some of the spectators in the banner crowd of 12,191 wondered whether to wait for Horace Ashenfelter to run away with the Larrivee two-mile, last trophy event on the starry Knights of Columbus program. An early start would beat the crowd, but Bostonians like to see champions running.

Ashenfelter got the most applause as he was introduced. John Joe Barry, the Villanovan who had entranced Bostonians by winning the Hunter Mile in the B.A.A. meet the year before, was given a hearty welcome. Osman Cosgul, a heralded invader from Turkey, received polite patter.

Crowd Sensed Unexpected

The attention stayed on Ashenfelter as the Olympic steeplechase champion covered the first mile in 4:28.6. Gradually the crowd sensed the presence of a challenger a tiny, black-haired runner whom the program identified as Charles Capozzoli of Georgetown.

With five laps to go this virtual unknown was closing on Ashenfelter — 15 yards behind. The crowd perked up when the newcomer was only five

CAPOZZOLI STOPPED THE CLOCK AT 8 MINUTES 55.3 SECONDS

yards behind and four laps remained. By this time the crowd was roaring—and so was Capozzoli.

On the backstretch of the 19th lap, Capozzoli burst past the startled Ashenfelter. Crowd noises reached a crescendo as the feathery Georgetown senior raced away to win by 50 yards. He stopped the clock at 8 minutes, 55.3 seconds, the fastest two miles ever raced by a collegian.

"Mom, I Beat 'Em"

A spotlight stayed on Capozzoli as he crossed the finish line, and stayed on him as he jogged a full circuit of the track. Charley played the part of a conquering hero, throwing kisses to the crowd and reflecting with his broad grin the exultation that he felt.

For a few minutes he disappeared, but a reporter found him in a telephone booth calling his family in Flushing, L. I.

"I lapped the Turk, Moma. I beat them all," he shouted into the phone.

Little wonder that Capozzoli was voted the William P. Kenney Memorial Award as the top individual star of the meet. The voting wasn't even close. That fantastic effort by Capozzoli was his only major indoor conquest. He was beset by illness and forced to forego competition for the rest of 1953, and never since that night has he shown the speed and form that whipped Olympic champion Ashenfelter. But Cappy never will forget that night.

Consistency: Bones, Thou Art a Jewel!

BY HARRY MOLTER *Christian Science Monitor Sports Writer*

Meet Harrison (Bones) Dillard, hurdler supreme.

The rhythmic grace of this sleek stylist, who keeps winning race after race on Boston Garden boards, is a thing of beauty. Here is a highly-skilled craftsman. Like the master jewel-cutter, Bones is a rare gem in a sport of specialists.

Harrison grew up in Cleveland—home town of another great Negro track star, Jesse Owens. As a youngster Dillard loved baseball. But the Owens influence at the time of the 1936 Olympic Games and the greater opportunities in track turned Harrison in that direction. He learned to hurdle by jumping over a worn-out auto seat in a vacant lot near his home.

Dillard has been winning hurdles races in the Knights of Columbus event since he first came here in 1947, flashing the bright yellow-gold spangles of Baldwin-Wallace College. All told he has won the K. of C. event six times including the last three years in a row. He has never lost as much as a heat in Boston.

Dillard has attained international acclaim for his 100-meters dash triumph on the flat in the 1948 Olympics at London, then proved supreme over the high hurdles in 1952 at Helsinki. He has aspirations to compete again in the 1956 Games in Australia.

Always in top condition, ever ready to cooperate with track officials and reporters, Bones is a man who wears his laurels modestly. He is a true champion, a credit to the track world. Watching him flit over the hurdles like a humming bird is a perennial thrill in any track meet.

HARRISON DILLARD

RED LIGHT
ON THE TRACK

By Jerry Nason
Sports Editor, Boston Globe

"My girl friend is so dumb," remarked Benny the Foot-Racing Filbert, "that she thinks a 'sleeper' consists of lower and upper berths!"

Benny, having been around the K. of C. meets in the Garden, sniffing the scorched planks as a regular patron, knows what a "sleeper" really is.

A "sleeper" is a generally unknown or underrated entry, his ability measuring up to his ambition, who puts a red light out on the track to warn the favorites — then covers it over with a blanket, so to speak.

If tonight's K. of C. meet produces a "sleeper", think nothing of it. The affair has produced more "sleepers" than the poppy field in the Land of Oz.

One of Smallest

One of the smallest runners to produce a king-sized upset was Charlie Capozzoli, super-charged Georgetown featherweight, and one of the largest was Campbell Kane, a towering sophomore out of University of Indiana.

Both exploded in front of national champions for K. of C. records on the Garden track — proving that a "sleeper" can come in either an economy-sized or premium package.

It is possible that no "sleeper" ever measured a man of such international proportions on a Boston track as did Capozzoli here last January.

Horace Ashenfelter was the tallest pine of the year and when he toppled, it was with a thunderous crash. He had broken the world record for the steeplechase. He had won the Olympic title. He had thrashed the greatest runners in

CHARLES CAPOZZOLI
Georgetown University
Winning the 1953 K. of C. Leo Larrivee Two Miles Run in 8:55.3, A New K. of C. Meet Record.

Europe. He had won the Sullivan Award, as America's outstanding amateur athlete.

New Meet Record

But it was little Charlie Capozzoli, obscure in the shade of this famous runner, who whirled around the Garden track in 8m 55.3s (fastest time ever made by a collegian) to beat both "Ash" and the K. of C. record.

Kane's long-strided triumph in the Cheverus 1000 in 1941 was sheared from the same pattern.

The big man of the time—holder of four indoor world records and virtually unbeatable — was the late and great John Borican. It wasn't so much a question of how much John would win by, but by how much he would break of Cheverus record. He undoubtedly was the world's No. 1 middle-distance runner of the moment.

Kane got there first, to both the tape and the record. With an enormous fighting effort, from the gun on, the Indiana student made Borican come to him, as they say in the track set. The neophyte from Bloomington unreeled a record race, 2m 11.8s, and in a dozen ensuing years that time has been bettered only twice in the Garden.

Beat McCluskey

Oh, the K. of C. has managed, somehow, to copyright some of the most gulpy upsets the Garden has known in any sport.

Remember little Johnny Follows, who looked like an Oxford undergraduate, and was, who talked his way into the Larrivee two mile race and outfooted the fabulous Joe McCluskey?

Or, George Guida, son of a Philadelphia cop, who'd come out of the

(continued on Page 8)

Mike Lee Reports

CAPPY WINS FRIENDS AND INFLUENCES PEOPLE

Charley Capozzoli, Georgetown's sensational runner out of Flushing, must have read Dale Carnegie's book on "How to Win Friends and Influence People," because everywhere he goes he does exactly that.

You know about his terrific performance in the Boston K. of C. Games up in the Boston Garden last Saturday night when he was clocked in 8:55 for the two miles, a record breaking performance for the tradition-studded Boston meet.

Well, another of the experts to fall under the charm of the wonderful lad from Queens, was Gerry Hern, sports editor of the Boston Post.

Gerry wrote:

"It was close to midnight Saturday before Charlie Capozzoli broke away from admirers and went to the public telephone booth in the rear of the first balcony of the Garden. He was dressed in the blue exercise suit he had put on immediately after finishing the most exciting running performance 12,000 spectators could recall out of the recent past. Around his neck was wrapped a white turkish towel with the hotel insignia prominently displayed.

"As he walked the ramp behind the box seats, people turned to stare—and then wave at him. He waved right back. Men grabbed his hand to shake it as he went slowly along the concrete alley. The people he couldn't reach by a wave, he threw kisses at. He laughed and laughed, enjoying every minute of his record-smashing two-mile run against the greatest runners in training.

"The new two-mile star is a personality, one of those unusual figures who lift spectators to waves of enthusiasm during and after a race. Charlie Capozzoli is not a shy, fumbling athlete who dreads the public acclaim. He is a star in the European tradition, who enjoys his triumphs just as much as the spectators.

"At the phone booth he borrowed a nickel from the Post agent because sweat suits have no pockets.

HELLO, MOM—Charley Capozzoli, Georgetown runner, calls his mother after racing fastest two-mile ever by a collegian.

"'I have to talk to my mother,' he said, explaining his call to Long Island. Outside the booth, his escort, Domenic Restaino, executive secretary of the meet, waited patiently for the excitement to subside. It didn't.

"'Reverse the charge, please, operator,' said the Georgetown star, 'I'm fresh out of money. Don't worry. They'll accept the call.

"While he stood waiting for an answer he hummed bits of song: happily accepted congratulations from a Garden usher and finally, he yelled, 'Hey, momma, 8:55—a new meet record. Yes, yes, I won.'

"There was a slight pause while momma talked.

"'Don't get nervous,' he said. 'I feel fine. And momma, listen to this'—and his voice gained in strength and joy—

MEANING: THAT'S TWICE HE PASSED ME WITHOUT SAYING HELLO!

'I lapped the Turk, momma. Honestly I lapped the Turk.'

"From the other end of the call—Flushing—the joy could be heard about that feat. The man called The Turk was Osman Cosgul of the Turkish Olympic squad who had finished fourth in the Leo Larrivee two-mile race.

"'Ashenfelter was second. Who was third? I don't know, momma. I didn't stop to find out. I was just five seconds off the world record. Five seconds, momma. Let me talk to daddy and Louis.'

New York Journal-American ★ Mon., Jan. 13, 1953—**17** ARY 18, 1953

Relentless Router

Unwavering Drive Makes Capozzoli Sure Threat Despite Lack of Form

By Barney Kremenko

In track, they're talking about Charley Capozzoli. He's the bony, 126-pound Georgetown senior who stole the Boston K. C. show Saturday night by upsetting Olympic steeplechase champion Horace Ashenfelter over the two-mile distance.

Perhaps even more astonishing than his decisive 40-yard margin was Capozzoli's time of 8 minutes 55.3 seconds, a new meet record. No undergraduate ever ran that fast before.

"Of all present day runners, he's the most amazing," said Bob Giegengack, Yale coach, after the race. "He has no form, he has no speed, he does everything wrong, and yet he wins."

NEVER QUITS.

How does he do it, then?

"Strictly on guts," Giegengack said. "He never quits. He's always coming at you. If you remember the race, at the end of a mile and a quarter, Ashenfelter held a 40-yard lead. Almost any other runner would have said to himself, 'What's the use of trying to chase him. Let him have it.' But not Capozzoli."

This is an appraisal of the determined Hoya with which practically all footracing savants agree.

"Don't think I underrated him," said Ashenfelter. "I knew he would give me the most trouble and perhaps beat me. I just didn't think he could go that fast, almost five seconds under nine minutes. When I heard the crowd roar, I felt that Capozzoli was moving in on me. Then when he raced by, there was nothing I could do about it."

CUT IN TRAINING.

Ashenfelter believes he is need of rest and plans to cut down sharply on his regular training routine this week.

"There'll be a hard workout tomorrow, but that's all. With the Philadelphia meet on Friday, I may lay off completely Thursday. On Wednesday, I'll work about three miles instead of the normal six or seven," he disclosed.

Despite the surprise occasioned by the outcome in the Hub, Capozzoli is hardly a Johnny-come-lately.

A former PSAL champion at Bayside High, Queens, Cappy was the man who shut Fred Wilt out of a place on the Olympic 5,000-meter squad. He outsped FBI man

CHARLES CAPAZZOLI
Winning in Hub
AP Wirephoto

Wilt for third place in the final trials.

At Helsinki, Charley turned in the best clocking of all the Americans, topping Curt Stone and Wes Santee, the other members of the three-man 5,000-meter group.

X-COUNTRY CHAMP.

After the Olympics, he turned in several snappy three-mile races in meets all over Europe.

The Georgetown whiz-bang is the present IC4A and NCAA cross-country champion.

Two weeks ago, in Washington, he won a two-mile special in 9:17. But that's a far cry from 8:55.3.

Firmly established among the upper crust of two-mile society now, Cappozzoli is bound to be heard from again and again and again. Certainly, the meet directors won't let him be forgotten. He was the most popular man in the Boston Garden after Saturday's race.

Capozzoli Breaks Two-Mile Record

A THING OF BEAUTY

The two-mile run was a thing of beauty, though not to the FBI Ashenfelter, who led for 19 of the 22 laps.

Villanova's Johnny Joe Barry stuck with the FBI man for the first seven laps, with Turkey's Osman Cosgul in pursuit. At this stage Capozzoli was running fourth.

Ashenfelter appeared to have matters definitely in hand, however. Capozzoli moved up to second place after nine laps, and Browning Ross, the ex-Villanovan who brought both the National 25 and 30-kilometer titles to the Penn AC last autumn, slipped into third, relegating Cosgul to fourth. Curtis Stone to fifth and Barry to sixth.

CAPOZZOLI CUTS LOOSE

They were in that order at the end of 18 circuits, then Capozzoli, 22-year-old New Yorker, cut loose. He glided by Ashenfelter so fast that the former Penn State star seemed to be standing still.

Of the others in the field, all save Ross and Cosgul had been lapped—even Stone, another erstwhile Penn Stater who beat both Ashenfelter and Capozzoli in the 5000 and 10,000-meter AAU championships last summer.

But it was a different story tonight. Capozzoli took those final three turns like a man just starting out. He was more than 40 yards ahead—a quarter of a lap—and Ashenfelter still was rounding the final curve as the lanky Hoya broke the tape.

Ashenfelter's fractional times—at quarter-mile stages — were 0:68.9, 2:16, 3:23.6, 4:20.6, 5:34.1 and 6:42.9. Clockers caught Ashenfelter at the finish in 9:03, Ross in 9:11.2, Cosgul in 9:25.7; Stone in 9:32.5 and Barry in 9:38.3.

Charley Capozzoli, who broke Greg Rice's Boston K. of C. two-mile record by 5.1 seconds last night, is the latest entry in The Inquirer Games Friday night at Convention Hall.

Chapter 14
"Illness Set-Back,
But Never Give Up!"

After the Boston Knights of Columbus track meet, we returned to Georgetown the next day by train. I was daydreaming of the races coming up knowing that Ashenfelter would be out to get me. He wouldn't let me surprise him again. How great I felt until the next night. While sleeping during the night, my roommate, Al, and I, began moaning. We became deathly ill with the flu, so bad that we ended up in the infirmary. That was the end of the indoor track season for me, my last opportunity as a Georgetown senior. I was never so sick in all my life. It took so much out of me that I thought it was the end of my running career.

Capozzoli Too Weak To Compete Thursday

Charley Capozzoli of Georgetown, this Winter's two-mile sensation, is definitely out of the Millrose games. Resting at his Bayside, L.I. home after the attack of flu that bedded him last week, the Hoya Olympiam suffered a relaspe and though he is feeling better now, he said today he is entirely too weak to run Thursday . . . the distance star will skip the Boston A.A. meet Saturday, too ...his next start probably will come in the NYAC Games.

The AAU launched a fund-raising drive with a luncheon at Toots Shor's yesterday . . . The goal is a half million dollars . . . Each of the AAU districts will conduct its own campaign . . . Big events of the Met. district AAU will probably be an April dinner at the Waldorf . . . Jeremiah T. Mahoney is national chairman of the drive . . . The luncheon also served to introduce the National AAU president, Douglas F. Roby of Detroit,

to most of the New York scribes. Should pole vaulter Bob Richards top 15 feet 1½ inches in Thursday's Millrose games, it will be the first time he has topped a meet record set by Cornelius Warmerdam . . . Both Richards and hurdler Harrison Dillard will be seeking their seventh straight Millrose victories . . . Fred Wilt hardly the one to remain idle spent Saturday night winning a 9:11 two-mile in Buffalo.

HE WON'T RUN. Charley Capozzoli of Georgetown U., this Winter's 2-mile whiz, is doing nothing more strenuous than looking over his scrap book at Bayside home. Weak after attack of flu, he'll be out of Thursday's Millrose games at the Garden.

Being so sick and unable to practice, I exercised in my room, doing push-ups, sit-ups, and stretching, as much as I could. Several months later, when feeling a little better, I practiced on the track with my teammates. The workouts became more tense. I then began to run in dual meets, both the mile and two-mile run on the same day. I was in excellent condition, setting records in both events, and ready for stiff competition.

"Never give up, do your best, win or lose, its love that really matters."

Chapter 15
"Capozzoli Runs 4:07.8 Mile."

"Run to Win—Do your best—Let no one tell you what you can't do!" These were my commandments in running. Never did I think I would be asked to break these rules, until my last race and appearance on the Georgetown track, my final appearance before the students.

It was a beautiful Saturday morning, especially for running. We were competing against the Baltimore Olympic Club and the Quantico Marines.

Frank Sevigne, our coach, called me aside, and said, "Let La Pierre win the mile. You are also going to run the two mile later and can win that."

This broke my heart. Besides, La Pierre was Georgetown's top miler. I wasn't sure that I could beat him anyway. Before the start of the race, I approached a Jesuit priest friend, Father Daley, who was there to watch the meet. I told him what the coach asked me to do.

"You run to win!" Father Daley said.

It was then announced to report to the start of the mile run. My mind was troubled. What should I do? Listen to Father Daley, or Frank Sevigne? My heart said, "Run to win!"

The gun went off. For the first two laps, I was in the pack, still wondering what I should do. We passed the half-mile mark in a slow 2:07. I then decided, "Do your best, run to win!"

La Pierre and I broke away from the pack, with our good friend and teammate, Ed Kirk, close behind us. La Pierre and I came down the homestretch with him having a slight lead. As we approached the finish line, I (Angels!) I beat him to the tape by a mere two tenths of a second, my time being 4:07.8, and his 4:08. It was the fastest mile run in America up to that time of the year. Kirk ran 4:15, his best time up to that point in his career. We were the best mile trio in college. I then ran the two-mile later that day. It was the fastest mile and two-mile run back to back by a collegian. On that same day, Roger Banister, with a pacesetter, ran a 4:04 mile in England. The following year Banister became immortal, breaking the 4:00 minute mile.

"Do your best, my son. Run to Win. Let no one tell you what you can't do!"

"Remember, its love that really matters."

Records Fall As Cappy & Co. Win Triangular Meet

Charley Capozzoli enjoyed his finest day on the Georgetown cinders last Saturday as he won the mile and two mile runs to pace the tracksters to a close triangular win over the Baltimore Olympic Club and the Quantico Marines. The final point totals were Georgetown 60; B. O. C. 59½; and Quantico 42⅔.

Cappy ran the fastest mile of the outdoor season so far as he hit 4:07.8, besting Joe La Pierre by two-tenths of a second. Joe pressed him with 220 to go but Capozzoli held on grimly and finally collared La Pierre on the final turn. Ed Kirk was a real surprise as he sliced eight seconds off his previous best mile time. Kirk took third position and was clocked at 4:15. In the two mile six man field, Cappy won easily with 9:13:3 with La-Pierre gliding in second. Third went to Jack Warner of the Marines and Gerry Foley picked up a point with his fourth place finish.

The sprints were taken by Cager of B.O.C. He won the 100 in 0:09.7 and the 220 in 0:22.0. Vinny Kelly was runner-up in the latter event, running 10 flat to take third in the century.

Capozzoli Breezes Over Mile in 4:07.8

Charlie Capozzoli of Georgetown University ran a 4:07.8 mile in a triangular track meet at Georgetown and equalled the fastest time recorded by an American miler in the last three years.

Capozzoli barely beat his teammate, Joe LaPierre, to the tape and still another Hoya, Ed Kirk, finished third. LaPierre's time was 4:08.0 and Kirk's was 4:15.0.

The only American to run the mile as fast as Capozzoli since 1950 is Len Truex, a former Ohio State Big Ten champion, who was clocked in 4:07.8 six weeks ago in the last meet of the indoor season six weeks ago in Milwaukee. The United States mile record

The 126-pound Capozzoli, a senior from Bayside, Long Island, said "I had to run that fast to beat LePierre. It was the greatest race he has ever run, too, you know. I feel now that I can do better than 4:07. I ran awfully slow first half."

"Cappy's first half time was slower than 2:07. He had to run the last half in beteer than two minutes. Bobby Jones, former George Washington High of Alexandria athlete, now a Quantico Marine, set the pace in the first quarter at 60 seconds. LaPierre led at the half with 2:07. Cappy took the lead at three-quarters with 3:08.

Forty minutes after his one-mile victory, Capozzoli won the two-mile in 9:13.3, the fastest time ever recorded on the Hoya track. Georgetown won the meet with 60 points to 59 1/3 for Baltimore Olympic Club and 42 2/3 for Quantico. A victory by the Hoya mile relay team in the last event decided the team championship.

Hailed for Boston Garden Performance

Capozzoli Fastest College 2-Miler in History But Also Holds Track Dream of '4-Minute Mile'

At Bayside High, where he started his remarkable athletic career, and Flushing, where he lives, they knew it all the time. Now the entire track and field world realizes that little Charlie Capozzoli is on his way to becoming one of the greatest international distance running stars in history.

Starting as just a guy who might make things interesting for Horace Ashenfelter, favorite in Saturday night's Boston K of C 2-mile whirl, Cappy bolted through with a phenomenal last quarter spurt. That mad dash so thoroughly upset Ashenfelter, world's fastest 3000 meter steeplechaser, that it left the Olympic champ 45 yards astern at the finish.

* * *

IN THE PROCESS of clocking 8:55.3, Cappy demolished the meet record by a full five and one tenth seconds. And it was no ordinary standard. It was posted 12 years ago by the great Greg Rice of Great Neck.

It was the best two mile effort ever by a collegian—indoors or out — and compares favorably with FBI-man Fred Wilt's American indoor record of 8:50.7. That mark seems in jeopardy this year with both Ashenfelter and Capozzoli rounding into top form.

The outdoor two-mile mark is held by Don Lash, who raced the route in 8:58.2—a full three seconds slower than Capozzoli—while winning the event at the Princeton Invitation meet in June, 1936.

* * *

THE FAMED RICE pulled a few collegians below the 9-minute mark indoors while whipping them, but even in those 'losing races did such stars as Lash, Wisconsin's Walter Mehl or Indiana's Mel Truitt come near the Georgetown swifty's time.

Mehl did it in 8:57.6 and Truitt in 8:59 as Ricethen a Notre Dame graduate—pulled them to their top efforts. Lash did 8:58 to win the Boston A. A. race of 1937.

* The meet will go down as one of the greatest in indoor history. Thrill after thrill roused the roaring crowd of 12,191 in the Boston Garden. Still the big stickout was the 5-9½, 125 pound Queens citizen. To him went the unanimous vote of the 14 track writers for the Bill Kenney Memorial Trophy as the meet standout.

* * *

THE CAPOZZOLI landslide

was no mean feat. His performance topped these of Ken Wiesner and Arnie Betton, who high jumped 6 feet 8¼ inches for a tie: Bob Richards 15 foot 3 inch vault, and such other meet records as Villanova Fred Dwyer's 2:11.6 for 1000 and Harrison Dillard's 5.6 seconds over the 45 yard high hurdles.

Modest as the Hoya senior is, he has an idea he has a chance of running a four minute mile, breaking Fred Wilt's world indoor two mile mark of 8:50.7. And trimming Rice's board floor three miler of 13:45.7.

* * *

CHARLIE, WHOSE home is at 163-17 25th avenue, Flushing, knows there'll be plenty of argument left in the spikes of Ashenfelter, Browning Ross, Turkey's Osman Cosgul and Curt Stone, whom he surprised in that order over the week end. He'll undoubt-

edly have to keep moving ever faster to stay ahead of them in the Millrose games at Madison Square Garden.

Questioning, however, brings out Capozzoli's thoughts on his mile and two mile possibilities. "Yes, I would like to try running a four minute mile some time. Most runners dream about that. And that 8:55.3 two mile might have been faster—it might have been a world record if I had realized I was in such good condition.

* * *

"I WAS BIT fearful of staying too close to Ashenfelter early in the race. He usually puts on steam around the mile mark. I just hoped to be able to pull up to him with three laps to go and then try outsprinting him. I was lucky to have it happen that way."

Capozzoli undoubtedly has nurtured big time mile ambitions from the time he was galloping that distance under handling of George Wright, the Bayside coach. His 4:22.9 registered in 1949 stands as one of the fastest schoolboy eight furlongs ever run.

* * *

FRED DWYER of Seton Hall High was Charlie's victim by a photo that spring day in Englewood, N. J. It's the same Villanova Dwyer who'll be among the favorites in Friday's Inquirer mile. Same time Cappy would like another one mile crack at PAL Freddie as well as Wilt, Ingvar Ericsson, Joe La Pierre and Don Gehrmann.

For the time being however, Cappy will concentrate on trying to become the world's greatest two miler.

Charlie Capozzoli, 125-pounds of track dynamite from Flushing, explodes along the home stretch as he steps into the finish string at the Boston Garden meet, setting a record of 8:55.3 in the Casey carnival. Cappy not only beat Horace Aashfelter by 45 yards, but turned in the fastest 2 miles ever clocked by a collegian. (AP Wirephoto).

Father Daley,
Our Dear Friend

Father Daley deserves a special page in this story and a special place in our hearts. He was not only a holy priest, but also a special friend. We trackmen loved him and enjoyed his warm friendship and love.

Was it a coincidence that Father Daley watched the track meet on Georgetown's campus, and my last race before the Georgetown students? It was Father who listened to my predicament and said, "You run to win!"

Was it also a coincidence that Father Daley was in Rome years later when my son had cancer and given six months to live? It was Father Daley who delivered our letter to Pope Pious VI in which we begged his holiness to pray for our son, John. Now, Father Daley, my wife, Donna, and our son, John, are all together. I call upon all three of them for very special favors.

Wilt Snares Trophy . . . G. U.'s Capozzoli in Top Performance

New York World-Telegram
The And Sun

New York 15, N.Y.

January 19, 1953

Dear Charlie,

Enclosed is copy of story I did x on you today. Hope it doesn't put you on spot. However, think you'll be on that anyhow, after what you did Saturday night. You didn't see it yourself. But you were strictly sensational.

I've been in track as an athlete, coach and writer 25 years. That makes me qualified, I think, to say that after what you showed in London last summer, in cross-country during the fall and against the fastest steeplechaser of all time, that if you keep up your keen ambition--that if you work the way Zatopek works for three or four hours a day--that you some day could quite possibly run a four-minute mile and break the world outdoor two miles, three miles and 5000-meter records.

Best of luck to you and stay as nice as you always have been. You may get beaten this week, next week or any time. But I'm sure you'll be the best some day if you really work for it.

Regards,

Lou Miller

D C

135

I May Run 4-Min. Mile —Capozzoli

By LOU MILLER.

Don't get Charlie Capozzoli wrong. He's a quiet, deeply respectful 21-year-old. Nevertheless, under cross examination, he admits believing someday he may run a four-minute mile, break Fred Wilt's indoor two-mile record and Greg Rice's three-mile mark. He allowed as much following his 8:55.3 double-mile stunner before a roaring 12,191 in the Boston K. of C. Saturday night.

Ordinarily you might h a v e thought the black-haired little 125 pounder a bit daft from circling thin clad in those drafts. Only you had just seen Bayside High's gift to Georgetown U. thoroughly subdue America's No. 1 Olympic hero, Horace Ashenfelter; Browning Ross, another Olympian; Osman Cosgul of Turkey and Curt Stone, national 5000-meter king.

Coming from 40 yards back of Ashenfelter with only four laps of the 160-yard oval left, the 5-8½ featherweight moved to within five yards of the pace setter next time around. Then he uncoiled a spurt that shot him into the finish 45 yards ahead of the FBI flash.

Wrecked Meet Record.

"Yes, it might have been a new world record," said Charlie. "Only, I didn't think I was ready to go under nine minutes this early."

The Hoya senior's clocking was fully five and one-tenth seconds better than the meet record Rice set a dozen years ago. Had he stuck closer to Ashenfelter through the early going he undoubtedly would have come close to Wilt's 8:50.7 world indoor two-mile standard.

The ace of Queens, N. Y., explains his strategy: "Horace usually pulls away at the mile mark. I wasn't going to stay with him that early. I hoped to be with him three laps to go, after he tired a bit. Then I wanted to try out-kicking him. That's the way it worked."

Mile Try Comes Later.

"I'll run anything Coach Frank Sevigne wants," continues Cappy. "I'm in the two miles this Friday night in the Philadelphia Inquirer meet and I hope to make it in the Millrose the following Thursday night in Madison Square Garden.

"But most any runner dreams of doing a four-minute mile. I'll try sometime, after I'm out of school."

Charlie has solid basis for his four-minute dream. Back in the spring of 1949, in Englewood, N. J., he ran one of the fastest miles in interscholastic history. He stepped 4:22.9 to edge Fred Dwyer of Seton Hall High. It was the same Dwyer, now at Villanova, who is one of the favorites in the Inquirer Mile, which also lists Wilt, Ingvar Ericsson, Joe LaPierre, Don Gehrmann and Warren Druetzler.

FOUR-MINUTE MILE? Clocked in 8:55.3 for his stunning two-mile victory in Boston Saturday, Georgetown senior Charley Capozzoli will seek a four-minute mile, after he gets out of school.

Chapter 16
Drake Relays, Des Moines, Iowa,
1952-53

In 1952, Coach Frank Sevigne entered us in several relay events for the first time competing in Des Moines. The team to beat was Kansas. We had no idea just how good they were. It didn't take us long to find out.

The gun went off. It was the start of the four-mile relay event. At the end of the first three-miles, our anchorman and top miler, Joe La Pierre was passed the baton with a substantial lead. Victory was ours for sure, until Kansas's young sophomore miler, Wes Santee, blasted out of nowhere with the speed of a cheetah, tore up the track, and beat La Pierre to the finish. Who was this guy that we never heard of? His anchor-mile time was 4:06! Phenomenal! It was wonderful to watch him run, even though we lost. His stride was different than any I had ever seen. He had great speed and was a runner's' runner. We congratulated him, his team, and coach. We became friends (better than enemies!), competed against one another in following years, and ran the 5,000 meters in the 52 Olympics at Helsinki, Finland.

We returned to the Drake relays the following year, 1953, again competing against Kansas's sensational team. Headlines and pictures appeared on the sport pages, "East meets Wes!"

Anyway, the gun went off, the start of the four-mile relay. This time we knew who Santee was! Our coach planned for us to build up such a big lead by the time La Pierre was handed the baton that not even the great Santee on a motorcycle could catch him as he did the year before. Ed Kirk ran the first mile, Carl Joyce the second, and I the third. Our coach's strategy worked. When I handed our anchorman, La Pierre, the baton, we had built up such a lead that Santee was sensible enough to settle for second place and save his energy for other events.

The next day we ran the distance medley. When I was handed the baton, this time I was the anchorman, we already had a big lead that it was impossible for Santee to overtake me. Even though we beat Kansas, Santee was the outstanding runner in the relays, having competed in several events, running sensational times. There was no doubt in my mind that he was the greatest miler in America, and one of the greatest in the world. For more about Santee's career, refer to "The Perfect Mile by Neal Bascomb."

"Run to win, do your best, its love and friendship that really matters."

Georgetown's 4-Mile Team Whips

Hoyas 200 Yards Ahead At Finish

Georgetown Defeats Kansas

Hoyas Win Medley by 100 Yards

Hoyas Humble Kansas, Santee

CAPOZZOLI'S EFFORT—Georgetown's star, Charlie Capozzoli, passes the baton to Joe LaPierre as the anchor leg begins. Cappy had about a 200-yard lead on Kansas at this point.

NO STRINGS ATTACHED—LaPierre winds up the race by nearly lapping an outclassed Missouri runner.

138

Hoyas Beat Kansas For Second Title

Des Moines, April 25 (AP)—Georgetown soundly defeated Kansas, the defending champion, in the university distance medley event at the Drake relays today. Bleak skies and a brisk wind prevailed as the two-day meet reached its climax with a 19-event program.

Georgetown's quarter of Vince Kelly at 440, Carl Joyce at 880, Joe La Pierre at three-quarters of a mile, and Charley Capozzoli at one mile, finished more than 100 yards ahead of Kansas in a creditable 10:06.

It was the second time in the meet that Georgetown made a run-away of a scheduled hot relay scrap with Kansas. In yesterday's four-mile relay, Georgetown also humiliated the title-holding Jayhawks anchored by the famed Wes Santee.

Santee moved Kansas up from fourth with his closing 4:15.2 mile in the distance medley, but Capozzoli's 4:17.4 gave him a 100-yard lead at the finish.

Kansas last year set the meet record of 10:01.8.

NEW YORK WORLD-TELEGRAM AN

three ICIA champs and a soph running together on the Georgetown distance medley. They are (l. to r.) Carl Joyce, 1000 king in 1952; Charlie Capozzoli, outdoor two-mile champ; Vince Kelly, from St. Augustine's of Brooklyn, and Joe LaPierre, outdoor mile and indoor two-mile ...

Herald Tribune—United Press telephoto

Charley Capozzoli, Georgetown's anchor man, hits tape to win university distance medley at Drake Relays Saturday. Georgetown's time was 10:06. Kansas, led by Wes Santee, finished second.

THE WASHINGTON DAILY NEWS, FRIDAY, APRIL 24, 1953—

Capozzoli and Santee Clash

DES MOINES, April 24—Two hot races get the 44th annual Drake Relays off to a fast start today under threatening skies and a forecast of afternoon showers.

The big events today will pit Capozzoli and Santee against each other in the four-mile relay while Stacey Siders and Santee will clash in the sprint medley.

The biggest fight of the relays is expected Saturday in the two-mile event when Wes Santee of Kansas and Stacey Siders of Illinois clash.

STAFF PHOTOS BY BOB LON

GLORY FOR THE EAST — Georgetown's great four - mile quartet poses with medals after winning Friday's feature at the Drake Relays. The Washington, D. C., school was timed in 17:20.6. Left to right: Ed Kirk, Carl Joyce, Charlie Capozzoli, Joe LaPierre.

Season's Best Times Cap Great Campaign For Hoya Relay Team

Georgetown University's distance relay team is back from California with two more trophies to wind up the season as the most successful quartet in the country.

Georgetown victories in the 2-mile Friday night in the Coliseum Relays at Los Angeles and in the distance medly Saturday night in the California Relays at Modesto were the fastest in the country this spring and capped a generally excellent week end for District area track teams.

Maryland won the Southern Conference championship for the third straight time and Catholic University moved to the top of the Mason-Dixon Conference. Only Navy failed to finish on top, taking fourth in the Hoptagonal Games at New Haven, Conn.

For Georgetown, it was Ed Kirk, Carl Joyce, Joe LaPierre and Charley Capozzoli, who turned in a 10:03.5 distance medley victory at Modesto Saturday night after Kirk. Capozzoli, LaPierre and Joyce had won the 2-mile in 7:34.3 at Los Angeles Friday night.

Carl Joyce (in front), and Charlie Cappazoli show the winning from they displayed as part of the four mile relay team which represented the Hilltop at the Drake Relays.

'Prayed All Year We'd Get Revenge,' Shouts Capozzoli

By Bob Asbille.

"I prayed all year that we'd get revenge," shouted Charlie Copozzoli after Georgetown's victory over Kansas in the Drake Relays featured four-mile event Friday.

Capozzoli, No. 3 man on the Hoya team, which won by 200 yards, grabbed Kansas anchorman, Wes Santee, and gleefully told him, "Boy, this is the sweetest race I've ever won. And look, I got a watch. Never won a watch for winning a race before."

Settled for Second.

Actually Kansas didn't try to make a race of it. "When we saw how behind we were, I was told to just run for second place," said Santee who last year picked up 60 yards near the finish to beat the favored Hoyas.

Joe LaPierre, who was the victim of Santee's surge last year said, "I knew I had him when I looked across the track with a half mile to go and saw that Santee hadn't picked up."

When the four happy Georgetown runners first lined up for pictures Santee came over to congratulate the victors.

Olympic Pals.

"Hiya, ya bum!" joked Capozzoli, who became a friend of Santee during the Olympic trials and the national collegiate meet last year.

Worked All Year.

Carl Joyce, the No. 2 man, admitted Georgetown had worked all year just for this race. "We should have won last year—anyway we proved we were good.

Ed Kirk, the No. 1 man, took a lot of good - natured kidding from his teammates since his was the only face splattered with mud from the

Georgetown and Kansas broke the Illinois stranglehold on the spotlight at times.

The Hoyas, who had humbled the dazzling Kansas combination in the four mile relay Friday, gave the Jayhawks another bitter dose of vengeance Saturday by taking the distance medley with something like the same smashing superiority they had shown in the four-mile.

Build Big Lead.

Their strategy was plain. The idea was for Vince Kelly, Carl Joyce and Joe LaPierre to run so fast and accumulate so much of a lead on the first three legs of the race that even Wes Santee, the great Kansan, couldn't hope to overcome it.

Georgetown did just that. Its first three runners set such a killing pace that Kansas was just about hopelessly distanced before the final mile began.

Hoyas Outrun Kansas Again

DES MOINES, April 25 (P).—Georgetown soundly defeated Kansas, the defending champion, in the University Distance Medley event at the Drake Relays today. Bleak skies and a brisk wind prevailed as the two-day meet reached its climax with a 19-event program.

Georgetown's quartet of Vince Kelly a 440, Carl Joyce at 880, Joe La Pierre at three-quarters of a mile, and Charley Capozzoli at one mile, finished more than 100 yards ahead of Kansas in a creditable 10:06.

It was the second time in the meet that Georgetown made a run-away of a scheduled hot relay scrap with Kansas. In yesterday's four - mile relay, Georgetown also humiliated the title-holding Jayhawks anchored by the famed Wes Santee. Santee moved Kansas up from fourth with his closing 4:15.2 mile in the distance medley, but Capozzoli's 4:17.4 gave him a 100-yard lead at the finish. Kansas last year set the meet record of 10:01.8.

Even so, Santee elected to try at the start. He was 140 yards behind Charley Capozzoli, Georgetown's flying anchor man, when the chase began and the smooth stride of the Kansas plainsman began eating into the deficit.

Eases Up.

Somebody apparently instructed Santee to ease up, however. The cause did appear hopeless. And through the last three laps Santee didn't run as Santee can run. He just breezed along faster than most milers could run but by no means fast enough to move in closer to Capozzoli.

At that, Santee's finishing mile was clocked in 4:15.1.

Georgetown's victory, its second vengeance triumph over Kansas, brought a clocking of 10:06, a mark which has been beaten only twice in Drake annals.

It was achieved with these approximate unofficial times; a 3:52 half by Joyce, three quarters in 3:09.9 by LaPierre and a 4:17 mile by Capozzoli. Kelly, who ran second in the opening quarter, was not timed.

EAST AND WES—Charlie Capozzoli (left), the Northeastern runner at the Drake Relays, poses with Wes Santee, the Kansas star, after Cappy had anchored Georgetown to a triumph in the distance medley. Georgetown, which won Friday's four-mile feature, was timed in 10 minutes 6 seconds in Saturday's medley.

Dark, Wet Weather and Tornado Scare Mark Opening of Big Show---

GEORGETOWN ROMPS IN FOR

Kansas' Santee Makes No Effort to Overcor

GLORY FOR THE EAST — Georgetown's great four - mile quartet poses with medals after winning Friday's feature at the Drake Relays. The Washington, D. C., school was timed in 17:20.8. Left to right: Ed Kirk, Carl Joyce, Charlie Capozzoli, Joe LaPierre.

STAFF PHOTOS BY BOB LONG.

California here we come.

Hoya Track Stars Take Off for Big Tests on Coast

Georgetown university's great relay team is lined up and ready to head for Modesto, Cal., where it will attempt to set a world record in the distance medley relay on Saturday. The quartet also will compete in the Los Angeles coliseum meet on Friday. Shown from left to right are coach Frank Sevigne ,Carl Joyce, Charlie Capozzolli, and Joe La Pierra as they boarded a plane Wednesday.

Chapter 17
"California, Here We Come!
Struck Gold In California!"

After winning in the 1953 Drake relays, defeating Kansas in the four-mile and distance medley relay, the big test now was to compete against California's greatest teams at the Coliseum relays in Los Angeles's Olympic Stadium. This time it was the two-mile relay event instead of the four-mile. We had the same teammates, but a change in positions and strategy, "the Sevigne plan."

It was a beautiful night, May 15th, a perfect evening for running. We were ready to take them on. Ed Kirk led off at the start, handed me the baton, and I ran my best half mile ever, 1:53, gaining the lead when passing the baton to Joe La Pierre, who increased it even more when passing the baton to our top half miler, anchorman "Carl Joyce!" Joyce took off like a scared rabbit and ran his opponents into the ground, another victory for the guys from back East.

Sevigne, our coach, did it again, another feather in his cap. This time he thought "all is well" and that the team would go back to the Hollywood Roosevelt Hotel, have dinner, and retire early, since we had to fly to Modesto the next morning to compete in the "Modesto Relays." This plan of Sevigne's was interrupted more so than ever before.

While I showered, one of my teammates called through the door. "Charlie, hurry up! There are three beautiful girls waiting outside whom we met and want to introduce you to them."

How could these girls be more beautiful than the ones we met a year ago in Long Beach, "the Miss Universe Contestants." I asked my teammate to count me out, since there were three girls and

144

four of us. My teammate insisted that I meet them. So I got dressed (couldn't go out directly from the shower) and went out to meet them. I was introduced to them, one by one, and thought maybe there's another Miss Universe contest going on. I was first introduced to Joan, then Betty, and then, and then, and then, Donna Dente! I went into a tailspin, took her by the hand, and decided not to go back to the hotel. Oh, my gosh! Was she for real? Forget Miss Italy, and all the other girls I met. This is the one I use to dream about when I was fourteen years old listening to ballads by Frank Sinatra, Perry Como, and Tony Bennett.

Instead of going back to the hotel, we accompanied these beautiful girls to the Helm's Foundation (prominent bakery company) where all the Athletes were invited for a buffet dinner. After that, the girls drove us back to the hotel (no hanky-panky) and said they would see us off the next morning at the airport. They showed up and watched the plane take-off. We were headed to Modesto to compete in a distance relay event. After take-off, I thought I'll never see Donna again or get her out of my mind. However, I got the name of her dad, Dante Dente, and then looked up her phone number and address in the phone book. Didn't have the nerve to ask her for it. We said "goodbye," but not forever as far as I was concerned. Would I ever see her again? The next day in Modesto, I called home. My mother answered. I said, "Mom! I met the girl I'm going to marry!"

Mom believed it, mother's intuition, but Donna knew nothing about my feelings towards her. She told her girl friends,

"He didn't even ask me for my phone number or address."

JOAN LYONS . . . Sodality . . . Campus Rumors Staff.

BETTY HAGGERTY . . . Sodality . . . Pallium Staff.

DONNA DENTE . . . Sodality.

145

Joan married my friend, Frank Flores, a champion USC track and field star in the "hop, step, and jump." Frank went on to become a "dentist!"

Betty married her teenage sweetheart, Bud Lacy, who became a "lawyer!"

Donna married "you know who, me!" Who became a "salesman!" I had to convince her to marry me.

Continuation of our California trip!

We went on to Modesto, winning the distance medley relay and were presented wristwatches by a beautiful young movie star. She was beautiful, but as far as I was concerned, Donna was on my mind and there was no one more beautiful than she.

After two years of communicating with Donna by letters, phone calls, and visits, I convinced her I was the one for her (poor girl). We were married two years later, January 2, 1955. We have four married children, sixteen grandchildren, and two great grandchildren. Sadly, Donna passed away from ovarian cancer December 21, 2001, to join her friend Joan who died several years before. Our grandchildren wrote a beautiful poem about Donna, "Grandma, with the Crystal Blue Eyes and Baby Soft Skin."

Since writing this story, our oldest son, John, recently passed away on Sept. 2, 2005, to join his mother and many other loved ones. Refer to the very last article in this story, "John Capozzoli Three Miracles!"

"In my heart lie these fond memories, like treasures of gold that one retrieves, of the good times and the bad, the joyful and the sad, we will always remember beautiful Donna with the "crystal blue eyes and baby soft skin." Nor, will we ever forget our loving son, John, and his godmother, Joan."

"Capozzoli Hopes With Hope to Win, But Loses!"

How could I possibly let the legendary Bob Hope down? Well, I did! During my last semester at Georgetown, in my senior year, I received a phone call asking me to please come dressed in my track gear to a hotel to meet Bob Hope. Wow! Was this for real? I rushed off to meet him. Several pictures were then taken of us posing as though it was the start of the race, fantastic! Unfortunately, I failed to get copies of these pictures which I regret to this day. To make matters worse, one of them appeared months later in Los Angeles, the day of the Coliseum Relays, "Capozzoli Hopes with Hope to win!" Guess what? I dropped out of the race, the one mile run, after being number one choice to win. Why did I? No one likes to give an excuse for doing something like that, but only an hour before, I ran second leg on Georgetown's two mile relay team. When handed the baton by my teammate, we were behind. I ran my heart out, the fastest half-mile I ever ran, and made up the deficit, passing the baton out in front to our third man, Joe LaPierre, who increased out lead even more. Our anchorman, Carl Joyce, scorched the track, bringing Georgetown in for a great victory, beating the best teams in the nation. What a night! A great victory in the two mile relay, dropping out of the mile run, and letting Bob Hope down. It would have been better had he ran in my place! God, however, has wonderful ways of helping up to get over our failures and depression. What do I mean by that? After dropping out of the mile run, I went to shower trying to figure out why I did what I did. Was it too soon after running my fastest half-mile ever? Did my side really hurt me (a stitch), or did I fear the competition? Whatever, I was depressed. As I showered, my teammate, Ed Kirk said, "Hurry, There are three beautiful California girls you must meet."

When introduced, I met the girl of my dreams, Donna Dente, fell deeply in love and married 18 months later. This was one of the happiest moments of my life.

Sorry Bob for letting you down, but thank you God for not letting me down.

"BELLA DONNA DENTE, THE GIRL OF MY DREAMS!"

"DONNA (DENTE) CAPOZZOLI, CRYSTAL BLUE EYES, BABY SOFT SKIN"

77TH ANNUAL OUTDOOR CHAMPIONSHIPS
MAY 29 and 30, 1953

Charley Capozzoli, of Georgetown, about to cross finish line for I. C. 4-A. record in two-mile run yesterday. His time was 9:00.2.

Jack Frank

Track

NEW RECORD- HOLDER — Charles Capazzoli of Georgetown, who smashed record for the Leo arrives two-mile, being clocked in :55.3.

stretch, with LaPierre beating the fading Dwyer. This race was run as the second and faster section. Georgetown's Ed Kirk, winning the first section in 4:18.2, got fourth in the final placings on time.

Capozzoli, going for the record he had promised, had Villanova's John Joe Barry for company for a mile and a half, then went off on his own. He ran the first mile in 4:28.8, hit the mile and three-quarters in 7:55.3, and had all kinds of records in his grasp in the final quarter. Cappy had run an 8:55.3, indoors, the fastest ever by a collegian, before he was derailed by a virus.

Top College Choice for 5,000-Meter Run

Capozzoli Named on Track 'All-America'

LAWRENCE, Kas. (AP)—The 1952 collegiate All-America track and field team was announced today by M. E. (Bill) Easton, secretary-treasurer of the National Collegiate Track Coaches Association.

The NCAA selections committee for the all stars was headed by Brutus Hamilton, of the University of California and a coach of the 1952 U. S. olympic squad; Elliott B. Noyes, of Dartmouth, and Easton, Kansas track coach.

One of the top selections was lean Charlie Capozzoli of Flushing, L. I., a product of Bayside High School and current star at Georgetown University. Capozzoli, a member of the United States team at the recent Olympic Games at Helsinki, Finland and NCAA and IC4A cross country champion, was selected No. 1 for the 5,000 meter run, ahead of Wes Santee of Kansas and Herb Semper of Kansas.

Little Lindy Remigino of Manhattan College, a surprise Olympic winner, was named third choice in the 100-meter dash behind James Golliday of Northwestern and F. Dean Smith of Texas.

The All-America squad:

100-meter dash: James Golliday, Northwestern; F. Dean Smith, Texas; Lindy Remigino, Manhattan.
200-meter dash: Thane Baker, Kansas State; James Ford, Drake; Art Bragg, Morgan State.
400-meter dash: J. W. Mashburn, Oklahoma;

Ollie Matson, San Francisco U.; George Rhoden, Morgan State.
800-meter run: John Barnes, Occidental; Henry Cryer, Illinois; Len Spurrier, California.
1,500-meter run: Joe LaPierre, Georgetown; Bob McMillen, Occidental; Leonard Truex, Ohio State.
5,000-meter run: Charles Capozzoli, Georgetown; Wes Santee, Kansas; Herb Semper, Kansas.
110-meter high hurdles: Jack Davis, Southern California; Robert Mathias, Stanford; Val Joe Walker, Southern Methodist.
400-meter hurdles: Robert Devinney, Kansas; Bill Johnson, George Pepperdine; Lee Yoder, Arkansas.
Shot put: Darrow Hooper, Texas A and M.; Fritz Nilson, Michigan; Perry O'Brien, Southern California.
Discus: Jim Dillion, Alabama Polytechnic; Sim Iness, Southern California; Charles Emery, Pennsylvania.
Javelin: Robert Allison, Navy; Milton Misfeldt, Oregon; George Rosemo, California.
Pole vault: Dick Coleman, Illinois; Bill Priddy, San Jose State; Gordon Riddell, Colorado A. and M.
High jump: Emery Barnes, Oregon; Walter Davis, Texas A. and M.; Fred Pratley, Utah.
Broad jump: George Brown, UCLA; Meredith Gourdine, Cornell; F. Morgan Taylor, Princeton.

Capozzoli Wins 2-Mile, La Pierre Mile in IC4A

By Herb Heft
Post Reporter

NEW YORK, May 31 — Joe LaPierre scored a smashing upset victory in the mile and Charlie Capozzoli followed with a runaway triumph in the two-mile to give Georgetown University two sensational victories in the IC4A track meet here today.

U. S. DISTANCE ACE - - By Alan Maver

CHARLIE CAPOZZOLI, OF GEORGETOWN, WHO'S BEEN RATED AS "POTENTIALLY ONE OF THE GREATEST DISTANCE RUNNERS AMERICA HAS EVER HAD," WILL BE THE DEFENDING CHAMP IN THE I.C.4-A, 2-MILE RACE IN NEW YORK, MAY 30.

IF THE I.C.4-A. MILE AND 2-MILE WEREN'T RUN SO CLOSE TOGETHER CHARLIE MIGHT SCORE A "DOUBLE"— HE RAN A 4:07.8 MILE THIS SPRING, ONLY 1½ SECONDS OFF THE RECORD FOR AN AMERICAN COLLEGIAN

K HERALD TRIBUNE, SUNDAY, M

Defending titleholders in I. C. 4-A. meet Saturday are this Georgetown pair, Joe LaPierre (left) and Charley Capozzoli. LaPierre is the mile champion and Capozzoli the king at two miles.

152

The All-American Board
of the National Collegiate Track
Coaches of America

having appraised the performance of
track and field men throughout the United States,
herewith selects and recognizes

Charles Capozzoli
Two Mile Run
Georgetown University

as a member of its

All-American College Track and Field Team
1951

Approved date _June_ 19_51_

C. S. Edmundson
President, National Track Coaches

M. E. Easton
Secretary, National Track Coaches

The All-American Board
of the National Collegiate Track
Coaches of America

having appraised the performance of
track and field men throughout the United States
herewith selects and recognizes

Charles Capozzoli
5000 Meter Run
Georgetown University

as a member of its

All-American College Track and Field Team
1952

Approved date June 1952

President, National Track Coaches

Secretary, National Track Coaches

Charley Wins a Big One

Charley Capozzoli of Bayside is congratulated by his father, Joseph, right, and Georgetown Coach Sevigne after winning the IC4A two-mile championship at Randalls Island Saturday. The Georgetown distance star ran the fastest two miles ever recorded by an American college under-graduate in collegiate competition. His time was 9:00.2 (AP Wirephoto).

Capozzoli Good U. S. Bet For '56 Olympic Games

By HUGH FULLERTON JR.

Since distance runners usually mature slowly, Charley Capozzoli of Flushing, a 22-year-old Georgetown senior probably will be America's best bet to beat the European distance stars in the 1956 Olympic games.

Capozzoli, a 126-pound wisp of a runner, already has run the fastest two miles ever turned in by an American college under-graduate—8:55.3 indoors last winter.

In the rain-soaked IC4-A meet Saturday, he knocked over two more collegiate marks for that distance as he was timed in 9:00.2 with no one pushing him. Both were set in 1949 by Penn State's Horace Ashenfalter, who went on three years later to win the Olympic steeplechase crown.

In the National Collegiate A.A. meet at Lincoln, Neb., three weeks hence, Charley will have a shot at the one remaining under-graduate mark—Don Lash's outdoor 8:58.3, set in the 1936 Princeton Invitational meet.

* * *

CAPOZZOLI was a member of the 1952 American Olympic team and, while he didn't win, he apparently learned a lot in Helsinki. His race Saturday was the second-fastest outdoor two miles ever run by an American college boy. It beat Ashenfelter's IC4-A record of 9:09.2 and Ashenfelter's record for all-collegiate competition, 9:03.9 made at Los Angeles.

If the weather and track had been better, or if there had been more competition, Capozzoli likely would have kept his promise to beat nine minutes and might have beaten Lash's record. As it was, he finished some 80 yards ahead of Villanova's John Joe Barry, who stuck with him for more than six laps.

Conceivably it could have been just the other way, as other events in the meet indicated. It's a matter of pace and Capozzoli, setting his own, judged it almost perfectly.

RUNS TO THE NEAREST EXIT . . . Georgetown's Charley Capozzoli snaps tape at finish of yesterday's IC4A two-mile championship. Cappy's clocking, 9:00.2, was fastest ever recorded by American college undergraduate in college competition and, natch, wiped out National Collegiate and IC4A records, both set by Horace Ashenfelter of Penn State. Manhattan scored 42 points to retain its team title.   AP Wirephoto.

New York Journal-American   ★★   Sun., May 31, 1953-**L-2**

"HE MAXIMIZES HIS OPTIMUM"

By JESSE ABRAMSON

New York Herald Tribune

MEN ON THE COVER — When the Editor of the I.C.A.A.A.A. Program asked Georgetown Coach Frank Sevigne for a photograph combining Joe LaPierre and Charley Capozzoli as I.C.4-A. Men of Distinction, he did not know, not being a seventh son of a seventh son, that they would finish in a photo a few days later in the fastest mile race ever run by an I.C.4-A. undergraduate. Probably Coach Sevigne didn't either.

In a triangular meet on May 2 on the Hoya track, Capozzoli was clocked in 4:07.8 and La Pierre in 4:08. The I.C.4-A. Collegiate record, not to be confused with the championship record, is 4:08.3, clocked by Louis Zamperini, of Southern California, in winning the N.C.A.A. title at Minneapolis in 1938.

Capozzoli and LaPierre are the only entries in this book currently holding two I.C.4-A. titles each. The former is the cross-country and outdoor two-mile champion; his teammate holds the outdoor mile and indoor two-mile titles. They will not, unless Coach Sevigne changes his mind, race each other in their last Intercollegiates. Each will defend his championship.

LaPierre is headed for one of the great mile races of I.C.4-A. history, for he will toe the mark with, among others, Freddie Dwyer, of Villanova, the No. 1 indoor miler of the year, who set an I.C.4-A. indoor record of 4:08.1 in Madison Square Garden last winter and will be out to regain the outdoor crown he won as a sophomore. These two, Dwyer and LaPierre, have had a vibrant mile feud all through their varsity careers in continuation of their prep school rivalry when they were teammates at Seton Hall Prep.

But it's little Charley Capozzoli, skinny little 128 pounder of five-foot-eight from Bayside High in New York, who most intrigues the I.C.4-A. family this spring.

He intrigued Brutus Hamilton, of the University of California, coach of the 1952 Olympic team, too. Charley unexpectedly made the Olympic team in the 5000 meters—unexpectedly because he had to beat our leading distance runner, Fred Wilt, for the third spot in the event.

The American threesome of Curtis Stone, Wes Santee and Capozzoli was in over its head, to be sure, against the likes of Zatopek, Mimoun, Schade, Chataway, et. al. at Helsinki. In the trial heats, Stone and Santee ran far behind their best, 14:42.8 and 15:10.4. They were shut out. So was Capozzoli, but he had the personal satisfaction of running the fastest 5000 meters of his life, 14:39.

That was something that appealed to Hamilton. All he could ask, as a coach, was that a fellow do his best. After the Olympics, in the traditional U.S.A.-British Empire meet, Capozzoli won the three-mile in 13 minutes 51.3 seconds, the fastest three-mile an American had ever run, faster than Wilt or Greg Rice, faster than England's Sidney Wooderson had ever run it. This performance moved Coach Hamilton to express his unbounded admiration of Capozzoli.

"Charley," said Hamilton, "comes as close to maximizing his physical potentialities as any runner I've even seen."

Capozzoli came back home better than ever. He was unbeaten in cross-country last fall, won the I.C.4-A. championship at Van Cortlandt Park by something like eighty yards, then set a four-mile course record of 19:36.7 at East Lansing, Mich., in winning the N.C.A.A. title by an even greater margin.

Even so, no one was prepared for Capozzoli's first important indoor two-mile test. He was up against Horace Ashenfelter, mature distance veteran and the Olympic steeplechase hero. The result was the biggest shock of the season. Capozzoli won by 45 yards in 8:55.3, the fastest two-mile ever stepped off by a college runner.

That feat intrigued Yale Coach Bob Giegengack, too.

"His form is awful," said Mr. G., speaking of Charley. "His arm action is floppy. He seems to be running on sheer grit. There he is 40 yards behind Ash, who is setting a murderous pace, 4:28.6 for the mile, and piles on another 65.5 quarter on top of it. Any other runner chasing Ash in that spot would give up. But nothing fazes Charley. He catches Ash with a quarter to go and runs him dizzy.

"When I saw Cappy run 9:17 two years ago, I said, 'That's his optimum. He'll never do better.' Then I see him run 9:10 and I say that's as far as he can go. The more I watch distance runners the more I'm inclined to throw the book away. From now on I'm not going to be surprised at anything Capozzoli does."

So, borrowing the coachly phrases from Hamilton and Giegengack, it can be said Charley maximizes his optimum.

Stricken by virus or whatever it was that was afflicting our runners last winter, Capozzoli's senior indoor campaign was arrested after that phenomenal 8:55.3.

But we have some idea of what he would have done from his remarkable racing this spring. The little Hoya ace hung up miles in 4:13.3 and

4:12.1 besides his 4:07.8; he ran two miles in 9:04.2, 9:07.4 and 9:15.3. The 9:04.2 is his fastest outdoors. Two years ago as a sophomore he had run 9:04.5 as runnerup to Michigan's Dorr McEwen in the N.C.A.A. That was the fastest two-mile ever run by a sophomore. Cappy's improved speed, strength and stamina are indicated in other ways. With his help Georgetown has the best two-mile, four-mile and distance medley relays in college circles this spring. When the Hoyas won the two-mile at the Los Angeles Coliseum Relays in 7:34.3, the year's best, Cappy unreeled his fastest half, 1:53.6, turning a 25-yard deficit into a lead the Hoyas did not give up.

The fastest miler and two-miler in the I.C.4-A. family this spring, Capozzoli had his choice of either title in the Intercollegiates. He couldn't run both under the I.C.4-A. timetable—the mile at 3 p.m., the two-mile at 3:35 p.m. He'll concentrate, therefore, on the two-mile, and Horace Ashenfelter's I.C.4-A. record of 9:09.2, set in 1949, and Don Lash's national collegiate mark of 8:58.3, set in the Princeton invitation of 1936, are his targets, weather permitting. Charley will have to do it alone. There's no one, on the record, within reach of him at his best.

Capozzoli is finishing his I.C.4-A. career in a blaze. That's the way it was when he was a 118-pound schoolboy. Always a contender but hardly ever a winner until his farewell school season, Charley won seven straight miles, climaxed by a come-from-behind stretch burst which brought him home a winner in 4:22.9. The boy he beat was Freddie Dwyer.

Behind the Keys
A Race To Remember
By GERRY de la REE

Saturday night up in Boston, Georgetown University's Charley Capozzoli and Villanova's Fred Dwyer scored outstanding victories in the Knights of Columbus track meet.

Capozzoli ran the fastest two mile ever turned in by a college athlete — 8:55.3 — and defeated Olympic star Horace Ashenfelter by better than 40 yards. He was later voted the outstanding performer in the meet. Dwyer set a new meet mark of 2:11.6 in winning the

Englewood, May 21, 1949: Charley Capozzoli (left) of Bayside High School wins Englewood Memorial Meet mile run in 4:22.9, as Seton Hall's Fred Dwyer collapses at finish line. A great race, a great picture by the Bergen Record's Steven S. Ditzian

1,000-yard run. Plenty will probably be heard from both boys during the balance of the indoor track campaign.

The mention of Capozzoli and Dwyer, however, recalls memories of a near-dead heat they ran one afternoon in May, 1949, at White Stadium, Englewood.

It was the greatest high school mile duel this writer has ever witnessed. It still rates as the fastest scholastic mile ever run in Bergen County and one of the fastest ever turned in by a schoolboy runner.

The slim, dark-haired Capozzoli, running for Bayside High School of New York, electrified the crowd that afternoon by edging out Dwyer, who was running for Seton Hall Prep of South Orange, in the amazing time of 4:22.9.

Capozzoli and Dwyer stuck with the field for the first lap of the race. The Bayside star then moved in front, with Dwyer following a few paces behind. Going into the final lap Dwyer made his bid, and finally passed Capozzoli on the back stretch.

For a short while it looked like the South Orange boy was going to take it. But as they broke into the home stretch Capozzoli put on a terrific burst of speed and literally ran Dwyer into the ground. He passed the Seton Hall star some 10 yeards from the tape and finished in front by less than a single stride.

Capozzoli finished strong, but as Dwyer crossed the line he collapsed, his body falling on the tape that the winner had just snapped.

The time of 4:22.9 was only 1.7 seconds off the national high school record of 4:12.2 set in 1934 by Lou Zamperini.

Track fans present at Englewood that afternoon knew they'd seen a race the equal of which they would possibly never see again in a high school meet.

Four years later these same two boys are among the top trackmen in the world. Neither is a Bergen County boy, but local fans who were fortunate enough to have seen that great mile battle of 1949 will long remember them.

By William Klemm—The Washington Post

GOODBYE, GEORGETOWN—Three great Georgetown University runners walk through the campus front gates for perhaps the last time. Left to right, Carl Joyce, halfmile; Charley Capozzoli, two mile, and Joe LaPierre, mile with their coach ,Frank Sevigne, behind them. They will compete in their last college meet in the NCAA in Lincoln, Neb.

Hoya Trio Finishes Collegiate Careers

Georgetown University
School of Foreign Service
Washington, D. C.

This is to certify that   Charles Joseph Capozzoli

was duly graduated from The School of Foreign Service, Georgetown University,

on   8 June 1953   with the degree of Bachelor of Science in Business

and Public Administration and is entitled to all the rights and privileges there-

unto belonging.

Dated   8 June 1953
NOT VALID WITHOUT SEAL AND SIGNATURE

Assistant   SECRETARY

Chapter 18
"Goodbye Georgetown,
May 1953"

"Exorcism!" During my freshman year, 1949-1950, we were kept abreast of every detail of a young child (lived off campus with parents) who was possessed by the devil. We were given blow by blow description of how it began the daily events, and the prayers of exorcism that took place. It was frightening, but true. It was so shocking that after being brought up to date each night by Jesuit priests who were on the scene, I was afraid to return to my room. My roommate and I were scared out of our minds one night when we heard the door to our room rattling. We convinced ourselves that it was caused by a draft in the hallway. However, we didn't sleep soundly after that.

After many weeks, maybe months, of frightening experiences for the child and parents, the prayers of exorcism were successful, thank God. We were told of the exact time when an Angel commanded the evil spirit, in the name of God, to leave the child's body at once. Our belief, from the description given by the child, was that the Angel was "St. Michael, the Archangel."

Georgetown's campus was quaint and beautiful. The dining facilities where we enjoyed having breakfast, lunch, and dinner, couldn't be beat. Upon entering the dining hall, we were greeted by a lovely hostess, and were served by waiters who wore jackets, white shirts and black ties (of course they wore pants too). The food was as good as could be expected, considering the many students served at one time (nothing like moms). The dorms were neat and clean. Believe it or not, we even had maid and laundry service. Was this the "Ritz

Carlton Hotel?" Being a runner in high school was very rewarding when I think about it. The track scholarship alone at Georgetown was priceless. My parents couldn't afford to send me there otherwise.

The buildings and landscape were picturesque, students walking from class to class, from building to building. There were student nurses strolling on campus in their white outfits, Jesuit priests walking with their breviary, silently saying their prayers. There were the tennis courts, the football field, McDonough Gymnasium, and the track where I spent most of my time. The scene was like a movie production in itself. Georgetown was not co-ed then except for the student nurses, who lived off campus. They added to the charm of Georgetown.

Several nights a week, my friends and I would take a walk across the "Francis Scott Key bridge" (Potomac River underneath) to Alexandria, Virginia. "Grandpa" would have loved this. On the other end of the bridge was a Howard Johnson restaurant where we would get a cup of hot chocolate topped with whip cream. For some of us, this was our treat and night out for the week, especially if we had a track meet coming up that weekend.

In May, 1953, it was now time to say, "Goodbye Georgetown," after having spent four years of learning, competing, and making lasting friendships. It had become my second home, the first being that of my parents. While it was a momentous occasion to graduate, it was also sad to leave, never again to see most of the students, the priests, the professors, and nurses who became friends. It was time to move onward, but where to? For some, it was marriage, graduate school, or military service. For me, it was law school (scholarship). So I retuned to Georgetown the following year.

Several teammates fell in love with nurses and married after graduation. Carl Joyce married beautiful Jean. Vince Cino married lovely Iona. Our team manager, Chuck Boyle, married charming Betsy (not a nurse). I had one date with a nurse, but that was as far as it went. She was very popular, sweet as could be, but I was in love with "Donna Dente, the girl of my dreams," whom I met at the Los Angeles Coliseum relays.

My parents, brother Lou, sister Marion, Grandpa, aunts, uncles, and cousins all came to Georgetown to attend the graduation ceremony. There were so many of them that they took over one floor of a nearby hotel. How proud they were. I was more proud of them. My mission was accomplished, the first in our family to graduate from college, the son of a shoe repairer, the son of modest parents, who encouraged me on to be something. "The love they gave, the sacrifices made," now came to fruition. How happy we were, but it was sad to say, "Goodbye Georgetown!" Thank you for being my second home. Thank you for the wonderful friendships! Thank you, mom, thank you, dad, most of all, thank you God! I only wish that I had tried harder and loved more while being with you, "Georgetown."

"Remember son! It's love that really matters, and in our heart it sings, so dream, my son, dream of wondrous things!"

Dahlgren Chapel

This is to Certify that

Charles Joseph Cappozolli

has been selected to appear in the
1952-53 Edition of

Who's Who Among
Students

In American Universities and Colleges

from

School of Foreign Service,
Georgetown University

This honor comes in recognition of the merit
and accomplishment of the student who
was officially recommended by the above
named institution and met the requirements
of this publication.

EDITOR

NEW YORK ATHLETIC CLUB

180 CENTRAL PARK, SOUTH
NEW YORK
Circle 7-5100

SEATING LIST

ALL SPORTS-OLYMPIC DINNER

WEDNESDAY, NOVEMBER 19, 1952

* * *

D A I S

Guest Speakers

Honorable Vincent R. Impellitteri
Frank Graham
Harry Wismer

Club Representatives

Harry L. Lindquist, President
Murray Vernon, Captain

Edward M. Swinburne, Chairman, All Sports-Olympic Dinner
Robert H. Goffe, Jr., Master of Ceremonies

Honored Athletes

Horace Ashenfelter, III
William Ashenfelter
Robert Backus
Richard Baldwin
Thomas Bane
Charles Cappozzoli
Henry Dreyer
Lindley E. Eberstadt
Samuel M. Felton, Jr.
James E. Fuchs
Silvio L. Giolito
Edward L. Jaworski
Rudolph Jesek
Robert F. Koehler
James La Rock
Edward L. Lee
Russell F. MacGrotty
Charles H. Moore, Jr.
Lindy J. Remigino
Curtis C. Stone
Fred L. Wilt

Charlie Capozzoli   Frank Sowa   Jerry Foley   Tom Flaherty   Ray Brophy

Star-Studded Track Teamsters Shatter Their

The 1952-1953 track season was well on its way to adding more names to the list of Georgetown's track immortals by the time the cross-country season was completed. The name of Charlie Capozzoli came to the fore as he won the IC4A five mile run and then went on to win the NCAA four mile race. Both marks he set were new records that seemed destined to stand for many years to come. The cross-country

team in the person of Cappy, Joe LaPierre, Eddie Kirk, Carl Joyce and Gerry Foley won three out of four dual meets. The indoor campaign was marked with Capozzoli's 8:55.3 in the two mile run by which he became the first collegian to run under nine minutes in the two mile event. This was not the only highlight of the indoor season though, for Joe LaPierre, subbing for the ailing Capozzoli, entered and

Joe LaPierre grabs the   The hundred yard sprint is

167

Carl Joyce   Ed Kirk   Vince Kelly   Joe La Pierre   Don Stonehouse

Own Records In Country's Foremost Meets

won the IC4A double mile crown clocked at a fast 9:08.9. In addition, Carl
Joyce won his third straight Boston
Lapham one thousand yard run and repeated this feat at the Philadelphia Inquirer Meet. All in all, the Hoya harriers tallied up quite a total score in 1953.

Outdoor Track Schedule

April	18th	Seton Hall Relays	Newark
April	25th	Penn Relays	Philadelphia, Pa.
April	28th	District A. A. U.	Georgetown
May	2nd	Quantico and Baltimore Olympic Club	Georgetown
May	5th	Maryland	Home
May	9th	Coliseum Relays	Away
May	9th	La Salle	Away
May	16th	Temple	Home

The Track Squad poses for their picture on the stage of the New Gymnasium. Charlie Capozolli is in the lower left hand corner.

Georgetown has had many great trackmen and will continue to do so. All contribute to many victories by doing their best.

Two of Georgetown's greats, who were victorious in individual events, as well as key teammates on the relay teams, were Carl Joyce and Joe La Pierre. They have since gone to their greatest reward and have finished their "final race of life!"

Several years after graduating and marrying Jean, a beautiful

168

nurse, who also walked the Georgetown campus, Carl was killed by an out of control car as he was leaving a weekday mass and walking from the church. He was deeply religious, a great person, and friend. Within the last few years, a street in Boston was dedicated and named after him.

Joe La Pierre recently passed away. Both men will be long remembered for many years to come by their loved ones, teammates, and Georgetown, our second home away from home for four wonderful years.

Carl Joyce

Joe La Pierre

Carl Joyce sprints for the tape

169

On the Oval

In back are Joe LaPierre, Joe Deady, Carl Joyce, Dave Boland and Tom Voorhees with Charlie Capozzoli in the foreground as they look into the future from the track oval situated on the tennis courts.
HOYA Photo—Harold Briggs

Georgetown Alumni Honor Capozzoli

Charles J. Capozzoli of 163-17 25th avenue, Flushing, Georgetown University's noted Olympic distance runner, receives a tablet from Frank Prial, left, president of the Georgetown Club of Metropolitan New York as Coach Frank Sevigne looks on. Presentation took place at the monthly dinner of the club in Manhattan. The placque given to the former Bayside High star is enscribed: "in grateful recognition of his athletic triumphs as a member of the 1952 Olympic Team, an extraordinary athlete, outstanding scholar, a credit to himself and to his Alma Mater, Georgetown University."

Boland hands the baton to LaPierre

Carl Joyce sprints for the tape

Joyce, Voorhees, LaPierre, and Boland training to break another record

"Dinner at the White House"

When visiting my parents in New York after graduation from Georgetown, my mom said, "You're wanted on the phone."

It was the Washington Post telling me I was invited to the White House along with other athletes to have dinner with the president, Dwight D. Eisenhower. Like a fool, I asked who would pay my way from New York to Washington D.C.

"You must," came the response

"I can't make it," I said and hung up.

My parents heard this and said, "Charlie, you know we would paid your way."

Don't ask me why I made such a rash decision. It was stupid on my part to deprive my parents of this great honor. Once again, God comes to the rescue. Another phone call from the AAU, asking if I would go to Europe for several weeks to represent America in track competition, all expenses paid! Off to Europe, Germany and Italy, I went, winning many races, bringing honor to our country and my parents.

I still regret not going to the White House. My apologies, Mr. President. I'm sorry Mom and Dad.

Chapter 19

Last Trip to Germany

After graduation, several of us trackmen had to remain on campus to continue training for our final track meet, the NCAA in Lincoln, Nebraska. Did we have our heart in it? None of us won our race. Rich Ferguson from Iowa beat me in the two-mile run. I don't even recall how I did. All I know is that we couldn't wait to leave Lincoln because of the unbearable heat. There were other reasons to leave (had to hide somewhere and get out of town fast for losing a race that everyone expected I would win and break a record).

"Learn to count in German!"

After leaving Lincoln, Nebraska, I was now aboard a plane with the American track team heading for Europe to compete in Germany and Italy. My first race was in Soligen, Germany, against Herbert Schade, their great distance runner, who broke the 5,000 meter Olympic record in his qualifying heat in the 52' Olympics. He finished third in the Olympic finals, Zatopek being first, Mimoun second, and Pirie fourth.

I'm now on the starting line with Schade. The gun goes off! It was 3,000 meters instead of 5,000. Schade took the lead. I learned my lesson the year before when taking the lead in the 5,000 meter qualifying heat in the Olympics. This time I planned to follow him (had no choice) as I followed Pirie in England, and Ashenfelter in Boston, until the final lap. Schade lead all the way, setting a blistering pace. With two (zwei in German) laps to go, he unleashed a tremendous burst of speed. It reminded me of that final lap against Fred Dwyer in high school when he did the exact same thing with

173

one lap to go, but Schade still had two (zwei) to go. I began talking to myself and to those Angels. I would have needed a fleet of them to catch Schade. Knowing there were still two laps to go, "do your best, my son," came to my mind. I was within striking distance of Schade as we were "approaching" the final lap (eins) to go. He picked up more speed, raised his arms to break the tape, but there was no tape there. We still had one (eins) more lap to go. He walked off the track thinking hc won. I knew that we still had one (eins) more lap to go. So I kept on going and won the race. I wasn't announced as the winner until later after a meeting was held by the track officials, Americans and Germans. They finally agreed that Schade, being German, should have known there were "zwei" laps to go instead of "eins." Don't laugh, Charlie! Remember that cross-country race in Virginia when you got lost and climbed over the chain link fence?

On we went to another German city to compete against more Germans and a Japanese team. Strange, huh? Not too many years ago we were at war against Germany and Japan. Our race was delayed because of heavy rain. Therefore, we went back to the locker room to wait until it subsided. We played cards while waiting. Fortunately we weren't playing for money. The nice polite Japanese beat me. To get even (joking), I beat them and the Germans in the race after the rain stopped.

Next stop was Berlin where the 1936 Olympics took place while Hitler was in power. I ran and won the 5,000 meter-run. Again, I found it hard to believe of what took place in Berlin during World War II. The Germans, and the Japanese, were wonderful people. When I arrived home from this trip, everyone wanted to know what it was like to compete against them. It was like anyone else, there was a handshake before and after the race. Win or lose, they were friends.

"Do your best, my son!" "Run to Win!" "It's love that really matters!"

Cappozzoli Wins 3000-Meter Run

SOLINGEN, Germany, Aug. 1 (P.—Charley Capozzoli, former Georgetown University Olympic miler, now a member of the New York A. C. ran the 3,000 meters in 8:30.2 and defeated Herbert Schade of Germany, who was disqualified when he stopped one lap early by mistake.

The American touring track squad dominated the International meet here winning nine of the dozen events before a crowd of 8,000.

Capozzoli Wins '5000' in Germany

HANOVER, Germany, Aug. 5 (P.—Charley Capozzoli of Georgetown University won the 5000-meter race in 14:30.2 and Mal Whitfield won both the 400 and 800-meter events before 20,-000 fans in a track meet here tonight.

Capozzoli Wins, in Berlin

BERLIN, August 2 (P.—Charley Capozolli, former Georgetown Olympic runner, now with the New York A.C. and on tour with the American Track and Field team won the 4000-meter event of an International meet finishing in 14:27.4.

174

Donnerstag, 30. Juli 1953

DER SPORT IM STADT-ANZEIGER

Nummer 175 — Seite

25 000 bestaunten das Laufwunder Bragg

Der schwarze USA-Athlet lief über 200 m mit 20,6 Sekunden Weltbestzeit für Kurvenbahnen und gewann die 100 m in 10,3 — Zehnmal Sternenbanner am Siegesmast — Der Belgier Herman durchbrach USA-Phalanx im 3000-m-Lauf — Doppelsieg von Fanny Blankers-Koen

Bragg beherrschte die Sprintstrecken

Je 100 m waren einer der leien Höhepunkte beim [...]ternationalen" gestern [...] Köln. Art Bragg siegte [...] 10,3 Sekunden überlegen vor seinen weißen onkurrenten. Fulterer [...]d dem Belgier Germaven. Bragg erreichte über [...]0 m die Weltbestzeit für [...]venbahnen in 20,6 Sekunden.

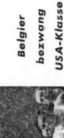

Belgier bezwang USA-Klasse

Einen europäischen Sieg gegen Amerikas Weltklasse erzielte über 3000 s der Belgier Herman (au unserem Bild an dritte Stelle in schwarzer Hose vor Capozoli und Dreitz (er (beide USA), die hie. das Feld anführen. Hinter Herman sieht man den Deutschen Herbert Schade (mit Brille), der sich nicht placieren konnte.

Chapter 20
"Last Trip to Italy, 1953"

After leaving Germany, we went on to Italy. Memories about Miss Italy in Long Beach came to mind (orange juice). On this trip, I had previously followed an Italian girl around in Turin, Italy, at a beauty contest, not realizing that she was trying to get rid of me instead of wanting me to follow her. She kept waving to me. I thought she wanted me to be with her, instead the waving meant "goodbye!" Live and learn (Italian ways).

We're now in Brecia, Italy, a very wonderful city. Of course, there are more beautiful Italian girls about the city.

"Be careful, Charlie, you'll be stood up again. Just be kind and polite. Don't follow any of them around, otherwise the Italians might blackball you from ever coming to Italy again."

As always, I went shopping in town to buy gifts to bring home to mom and dad. I went to a leather goods store, had a brief conversation with a sales lady. I said "goodbye" before she did. Ha! Ha! I'll show them!

The following day, the big track meet is getting underway. I'm to run the 3,000 meters, again not knowing who their best Italian runner was. The gun went off! I took the lead and ran my heart out. Hey! I wanted to show these Italians what an Italian from America could do. Maybe Miss Italy might be watching, or the other one I followed around at the beauty contest. I'll show them. Next time they'll show me more respect (joking, of course). I was in great shape, felt very confident and really wanted to perform my very best for the

176

Italian spectators. I won and was only four seconds off the world's record. Had no idea that I was going that fast.

The next morning, while having breakfast at the hotel, the maitre 'd came to our table and said, "There are five Italian girls here with flowers for Mr. Capozzoli."

Oh! What do I do now? Meet them dummy! I did, and thanked them for the flowers.

One of them was the pretty sales lady I met at the leather goods store. She invited me and my teammates to her home that night for a social gathering. We went, had a wonderful time, took pictures the following day, and then said a tearful goodbye. They were lovely young ladies whom we appreciated meeting.

"My son, run to win, do your best, dream of wondrous (Italian girls?) things."

Mike Lee Reports

MORE HONORS FOR CAPOZZOLI

Charley Capozzoli of Flushing, one of the world's best distance runners, will receive a certificate designating him as the top runner of Italian extraction in ceremonies at the Plaza Hotel, Jersey City, Saturday night . . . the presentation will be made by the Unico National of which Dr. D. M. Nigro is chairman . . . other top athletes to be honored are Rocky Marciano, Carl Furillo, Billy Martin, Phil Cavaretta, and Frank Crosetti. . . Winners were chosen on a ballot of sports writers and sports-casters.

Cappy makes a hit with Italians on both sides of the Atlantic . . . when he ran in Italy recently, shattering the Italian 3,000-meter record by six seconds

FOR THE FIRST TIME I DON'T FEEL LIKE RUNNING!

with an 8:21 clocking, 30,000 fans at the stadium cheered him wildly as he slowly circled the track after the time was announced . . . five bouquets of flowers from five different girls were delivered to Cappy's hotel . . . and knowing what a modest lad he is, I know he must have blushed with all this floral attention.

Capozzoli Runs
3000 M. 8:21'

BRESCIA, Italy, July 24 (AP)
A touring American track and field squad made a clean sweep of all 11 events in a meet against an Italian team at Brescia Stadium tonight.

The loudest cheers of the night went to Charlie Capozzoli, who turned in an 8:21 clocking for 3000 meters. The time was 4 seconds off the world record.

apozzoli Taking Time Out After Wowing 'em in Europe

By DON RODDA

Charley Capozzoli, Flushing's runnin' man, is taking a deserved rest pending resumption of training nxt month for upcoming cross-country and indoor track and field seasons.

Dark, slightly-built Cappy, a five-eight featherweight, can use a little relaxation. He's had an active year, barring a three-week bout with the virus during the last indoor season, and is just in from a four-week European tour with a nine-man AAU squad.

Running in Germany and Italy, Cappy was never out of the money. He won five of eight races — from 1,500 to 5,000 meters; took two seconds, and a third. Besides the best Germany and Italy sent against him, Charley's opposition included Warren Dreutzler and his New York A. C. teammate, Horace Aahenfelter.

In Berlin, Charley stepped the 5,000 in 14:27.4, just 8/10 seconds off the American record. He was a big hit in Italy, home of his grandparents. Capozzoli's running in a 3,000-meter event — plus his ancestry — won him an ovation from 5,000 Brescia fans. And after a Turino meet, delighted Italian officials embraced and kissed their fleet paesano from America.

The Germany-Italy junket was Cappy's third trip abroad. As a Georgetown sophmore he ran in Scandinavia in 1951, and last year, as a member of the Olympic team, displayed his talents in Finland, England, and other countries.

Cappy made the Olympic team by running third behind Curtis Stone and Wes Santee in the trials. He was runner-up to Stone in the 5,000 in the 1952 Nationals, nosing out Fred Wilt.

Capozzoli, although he placed seventh in the Olympic 5,000 meters at Helsinki, so impressed Coach Brutus Hamilton that the Yank mentor publicly praised the Flushingite's competitive spirit. A short time later, in London, Charley proved the accolade was appropriately bestowed by running three miles in 13:51.8, to crack Greg Rice's 14-minute American record.

Browning Ross as he set an intercollegiat mark. In the 1951 NCAA championships, Capp set a two-mile sophmore record of 9:04.5. Whil at Bayside High School ('49), Charley was cit and state one-mile kingpin.

Charley won't run any more until the Senio Met and National AAU cross-country event They'll be tune-ups for his first indoor meet the Washington Evening Star games in January.

The wiry little Flushingite in September i due to return to Georgetown, from which he wa graduated last June, for pre-law studies. As he used up his four years intercollegiate eligibilit; he'll henceforth compete for New York A. C.

Such is Cappy's devotion to the track, he not completely give it up during his vacation He exercises continually, doing push-ups, sit-up and bends each morning and before he turn in at night. For heavier work, he hoists metal last used by his dad, Joseph Capozzol who is a shoemaker.

"I've been doing it since I was 11 years old, grins the likeable youngster. "I wouldn't fee right without exercising."

When he's not doing odd jobs around th house, Charley likes to listen to music. He ha a nice collection of wax records to go with th cinder-track ones he's set.

CHARLEY CAPOZZOLI

Chapter 21
"Home From Europe"

After a very successful trip in Europe, it was wonderful to return home to be with my family. We talked about the trip, especially about Italy, where grandpa was born and where dad spent 15 years of his childhood. Couldn't understand why they would leave such a beautiful country, but they did. America offered freedom of speech, religion, and opportunities.

The first thing mom cooked for me was spaghetti and meatballs. Oh! Was it good! Far better than anything I had in Italy. That's the truth! The following meals mom made for me was the "leg of lamb with a baked potato, rice, and gravy poured over it." Then, "the roast beef, mashed potatoes, red cabbage, and "a' jus" over it." Am I making you hungry? What a gift to have a mom who could cook as she did.

Dad now discussed with me important matters, such as my first year at law school, becoming an attorney and training for the '56 Olympics. This was his dream. Mine too!

"Son, don't get serious with women right now. Concentrate on law school and the '56 Olympics," he said.

His advice was well taken, but I had met Donna Dente a few months before in California, the girl that I told mom I was going to marry. Dad knew I was in love and there wasn't anything one could do about it, except Donna.

Donna came to New York with her mother a few weeks before I was to leave to Georgetown. Mom and dad were kind and courteous to them. I could see in mom's eyes that my future was about to change.

They had always hoped that I would eventually marry a girl who lived nearby. "Love is love" and no one can change it. Donna went back to California wondering, "Is this Charlie crazy?" Meaning, she wasn't all that interested in me. I said to myself, "You and these Italian girls. Another put down!"

First year of law school, I returned to Georgetown (scholarship), began law school, and prefecting. I had to prefect to maintain my track amateur athletic status. Otherwise, I would have been declared a professional. Once declared a professional, your track career was over. There was no professional track in those days. What a pity. I prefected a group of students, some trackmen, on one floor of a dorm. It meant checking their rooms at 7:00, 9:00, and 11:00 p.m. (lights out). We said a Rosary each night in the dorm's hallway. Every student was welcomed to join in.

Throughout the first year of law school, I communicated with Donna by letters and phone calls. During Christmas recess, Donna came back to New York alone with her parent's approval. Her mom liked my parents and let Donna come back to survey the area, me! once again. While she was with us, I had received three requests to compete in races, one in Soa Paulo, Brazil, one in England, and the third, "the Sugar Bowl" in New Orleans. I selected "the Sugar Bowl" thinking it's the closest and I could quickly return to be with Donna.

"Santee vs. Capozzoli, the Sugar Bowl!" What did I do? I didn't know the great "Wes Santee" was waiting to make mincemeat out of me in the mile run. Oh, well, "do your best!" I went alone, no coach, just me. I spent the night at a Georgetown student's home as his guest, but couldn't sleep (excuse #1). The next day, we're on the starting line. Hey! Santee's a lot taller than me, (excuse #2). His Angels must be taller than mine! The gun went off. Wow! I would have been better off playing in the "Sugar Bowl" on one of the football teams as a lineman.

I'm not sure of the details of the race, but with three hundred yards to go, I blasted away (too soon and not enough). Santee was on my tail. What do I do now? Keep on going! Maybe he'll tire? Like a bolt of lightning, he passes me, and wins in the great time of 4:04. My time was ok. Someone clocked me in 4:08. Santee's great coach, M. E. (Bill) Easton, a wonderful person, asked me why I sped up with three hundred yards to go?

"Wouldn't you with a big guy like Santee chasing you?" I said.

A full page colored picture of Santee about ready to pass me appeared in a "sports magazine." I can't locate the written article that went with it. Wonder why?

Santee was a good friend and a runner's runner. He was truly one of the greatest in the world, though Roger Banister was the first to break the four-minute mile. I enjoyed watching Santee run, especially if it was against someone else and not me! You can read about Santee and Banister's life in a recent publication, "The Perfect Mile, by Neal Bascomb."

"God bless you, Wes!"

My running career was now coming to an end not because of being beat by Santee, but because of health problems. Several months later while practicing at Georgetown, coach Frank Sevigne called me aside saying that I was breathing very heavily and asked if I felt ok. I didn't! So I took a trip to New York to be examined by our family doctor. He called my parents to tell them that I had developed a serious respiratory ailment and must quit running if they want me around. I didn't listen to the doctor's orders and continued to run, only to lose races and to find my breathing getting more difficult under normal conditions.

After successfully completing the first year of law school, I gave up my scholarship, against the advice of the dean, and volunteered into the Army, requesting to be drafted in California (near where Donna lived). At the end of basic training, I married "the girl of my dreams, Donna Dente!" I continued running while married and in the Army, but no longer had the health to be able to contend with the great champions of the day. Was I sad because of this? Of course, but I was now married to "Donna, my greatest prize," whom I met at the Coliseum Relays eighteen months before. We had four beautiful children, and later eighteen grandchildren with more on the way, God willing. While running was great and rewarding, I thank God for having met Donna and for our family. There is nothing more important than ones' family. The very first chapter begins with "the family!" "It's the family and love that really matters!"

"Remember, my son, do your best, win or lose, dream of wondrous things, its love that really matters!".

Cappy Is Happy, 2d To Santee

By LOU MILLER.

Charley Capozzoli, visiting his folks in Bayside over the weekend, was asked how he felt about being beaten 50 yards by Kansas' Wes Santee in the sensational 4:04.2 Sugar Bowl Mile last Thursday. It might have been like asking a hit-and-run victim how it felt losing a decision to a truck.

It was strange, therefore, to hear Cappy say, "I feel very good about that race. I hadn't trained hard because it was too early and there's a long season ahead. If without preparation I could do 4:08, which some unofficial timers gave me, then I am encouraged into believing I might run some really fast miles this year.

"Santee is a marvelous runner as well as a wonderful guy. I feel sure he'll run the four-minute mile. But after our race in New Orleans I feel I might have a chance against him. The Lord willing, I might be with Wes the day he runs four minutes!"

Wants Big Invitations.

Capozzoli, whose 13:51.8 two years ago was the fastest outdoor three miles ever by an American, hopes to get into the big invitation miles this winter. He certainly would seem qualified, off that Sugar Bowl performance and last year's

184

by RED SMITH

THE kids at Bayside High School on Long Island ran the class mile in November. The day was raw and cold and clammy and gray, the color, temperature, and consistency of an oyster on the halfshell. The class mile at Bayside was a standard event in the physical education program, a competition among freshmen, sophomores, juniors, and seniors on a concrete track. There was a howling wind. In the delay before the start, a shivering freshman cowered on the lee side of a leafless tree for protection against the gale. He was a skinny kid, maybe 116 pounds, fully dressed, and he wasn't fully dressed. He wore a bathing suit, because he owned no track togs.

He won the race. His time was 5:17, which would be pretty good for a fat man with varicose veins. It did not suggest that there were any potential champions among the undergraduates at Bayside. There was one, though. The skinny little freshman who won was Charley Capozzoli.

This is a piece about Charley Capozzoli, a good foot racer. It isn't, strictly speaking, a sports piece. It's a piece about an exceptional young man who happens to be able to run very well. He'd be just as well worth writing about if he couldn't run at all, but of course nobody would write about him then because no sports writer would ever hear of a little guy like that.

Charley is a postgraduate student in law at Georgetown University. He is twenty-two years old, going on twenty-three; he weighs 133 pounds, stands five-feet-eight, and his dark, hollow-cheeked face is lighted by a smile that can only be described as sweet.

In the sleeveless camisole and half-column britches that serve him as evening wear, he looks slightly smaller than ninety-five cents' worth of liver. The kids at Georgetown have another way of describing him. They call him "two legs and a heart."

He is a daily communicant, not the only one at Georgetown, but perhaps the only one who can find enough hours in a day to attend Mass, wrestle *Blackstone's Commentaries* to a decision, and

still get out before dark to run miles along the Potomac's bank. He runs because of a sincere conviction that every man should employ as well as he can the gifts his Maker has given him, and he accepts victory or defeat humbly as the will of God.

If this is a picture of a paper saint, a prissy little lay preacher, then it's entirely inaccurate. Charley Capozzoli is all whalebone and whipcord and effort, as fierce a competitor as could be found in any sport. He is also a quiet, gracious, charming young man who does his best with such stirring resolution that just to watch him is a small inspiration.

Watching him inspired Brutus Hamilton, coach of the 1952 United States Olympic track and field team, to language of a sort seldom heard except from a Madison Avenue advertising executive.

"Capozzoli," Brutus said, "maximizes his potential better than any other man I have ever seen in the sport."

ORDINARILY sports stories don't concern themselves with an athlete's religion but Charley's faith is so much a part of him that the least discerning must be aware of it. There was one occasion when he must have thought for a moment that he was being teased about it by Horace Bigelow, of the New York Athletic Club. (No longer eligible for undergraduate competition, Capozzoli now runs in the N.Y.A.C. colors.)

"I can tell you," Bigelow offered, "an easy way to knock a second or two off your time in any race. It's about that scapular you wear—"

Charley stiffened. "Nothing could make me leave that off, Mr. Bigelow."

"I'm a scapular man myself," Bigelow assured him, "but this one bounces up and hits your nose with every stride. Wear it, Charley, on a shorter chain."

In spite of his bristling 5:17, winning the class mile at Bayside made a track man out of this small son of a Flushing, L. I. cobbler. He had fun running in high school, and he improved his original clocking more than somewhat. Even as a small boy, Charley Capozzoli was

learning to maximize his potential. Competing with his team in the Seton Hall Relays in New Jersey, he met a Father Parsons, who talked up the attractions of Georgetown. "It sounded good," Charley says. So he enrolled and got his Bachelor of Science degree.

He had finished his junior year when he got a chance to maximize first-hand for Brutus Hamilton. This was in Helsinki in July, 1952. Charley had made the Olympic team by finishing third at 5,000 meters in the final American tryout in Los Angeles. Curtis Stone had won that race in 14 minutes, 27 seconds, three seconds faster than the American record, with Wes Santee of Kansas second.

The United States never has won an Olympic 5,000, never really came close except in 1952 when Oregon's Ralph Hill ran a virtual dead heat with Finland's Lauri Lentinen, who was declared the winner after judges had debated for an hour. Our guys don't feel, as the Finns do, that a man can't rightly call himself a runner unless he crossed the county line in a race.

(An old gaffer in Helsinki overheard mention of Andy Stanfield, the sprinter. "Stanfield?" he asked. "Who is he?" The American champion, he was told. The old guy blinked. "How can he be champion to run 200 meters?" he asked. "He should run anyway five kilometers.")

AS it turned out, America didn't get into the 5,000-meter final in 1952. Stone was eighth and out in his heat. Santee was next to last in his. Capozzoli ran over his head to be seventh—the first five qualified—in 14 minutes, 39 seconds. On comparative times, he walloped Santee and Australia's John Landy, the two milers in the world today, who shoot the four-minute mile every time they start.

In Helsinki, Capozzoli trained with big fellows like Bob McMillen, of Occidental College, and they suggested that he was taking a lot out of himself by over-striding. Charley didn't risk changing his style for the Olympics, but when he flew from Helsinki to London for

Charley Capozzoli: the kid from Bayside keeps maximizing

Kid Alpert photo

the British Empire Games he decided to experiment.

"I just tried to relax," he says. "I'd never known I was over-striding; it was just natural, I guess. In London I kind of gathered myself and I didn't seem to get so tired. I seemed to have more left for a finishing kick. I could lengthen my stride then and get something out of it."

What he got out of it was the fastest three miles ever run by an undergraduate anywhere. He won in 13 minutes, 51.8 seconds from a field that included, among others, Gordon Pirie, the hasty London bank "clerk" who had been fourth in the Olympic 5,000.

Still maximizing like crazy, Charley set out in the winter of 1953 to run the glamour boys of indoor track plumb down to their knees. In the Knights of Columbus Games in Boston he peeled off two miles in 8 minutes, 55.4 seconds, swiftest time ever made by a college runner in this country.

Then a virus infection knocked him out, ruining the rest of the season for him. Save for his illness, he might very well have won the James E. Sullivan Memorial Award as America's outstanding amateur athlete. As it was, only one candidate received more first-place votes than he.

When the winter season of 1954 opened, 'flu bugs were still, or again, using Charley as their legal address. Stopping over in New York on his way to the Boston K. of C. meet, he confessed that he felt terrible. He hadn't been eating much, but the resident bacilli had enjoyed two meals of penicillin that week. He was asked why he didn't scratch from the meet.

"Those people up there are depending on me," he said, "and I owe them so much." He honestly believes that he incurs a new debt of gratitude every time his entry is accepted.

It was suggested to him that distance runners don't usually reach a peak until they're twenty-nine or thirty years old. At the rate he's been improving, there's no estimating how many records he might destroy in the next half-dozen years.

"I'd like to keep running as long as I can," he said seriously. "The more you run, the more obligations you have." This was a fortnight after this year's K. of C. Games. He felt he'd shaken off the virus and he was on his way to the Boston A.A. meet. An acquaintance wished him good luck up there.

"Thank you," he said, "I hope so. I hope I can help Horace Ashenfelter. If he has somebody to push him this week, I think he has a real good chance to break the world record."

(He never mentioned beating Ashenfelter.)

Sullivan award, 1953,
Outstanding Amateur Athlete

In December, 1953, while attending law school, I was nominated as one of eight athletes for the "James E. Sullivan Award," per details as per news article and letter received from Jack Keville, an executive with Celanese Corporation.

In the final tally, Major Sammy lee, two-time Olympic Platform Diving Champion in the 1948 Olympics, was the winner. Second was Pat McCormick, who won two Olympic Springboard-Platform medals in the 1952 Olympics. I was third in the final tally with 123 first place votes (didn't win an Olympic Medal!).

Lee Named Sullivan Award Winner; Pat McCormack 2nd, Capozzoli 3rd

Major Sammy Lee of the Army Medical Corps, two-time Olympic platform diving champion, is the 1953 winner of the James E. Sullivan Memorial Trophy.

This award is presented annually by the Amateur Athletic Union of the United States to "the athlete who, by performance, example and good influence, did most to advance the cause of good sportsmanship during the year."

A final tally yesterday showed Major Lee, whose home is in Pasadena, Calif., to have been first choice on 247 of the 631 ballots cast by the nation-wide tribunal of sports authorities participating in the 24th annual Sullivan Award poll.

* * *

ON A 5-3-1 COUNT of first, second and third place votes, the 33-year-old graduate of Occidental College, now on Army duty in Korea, amassed a total of 1,676 points.

This gave him a substantial edge over the seven other athletes who figured in the final balloting for the Sullivan Trophy, regarded as the top honor that can be bestowed on an amateur athlete in this country.

Major Lee, runnerup to Horace Ashenfelter in last year's Sullivan Award balloting, is the first diver and also the oldest athlete ever to win the prized trophy. He also is the first athlete of Oriental descent to be so honored. He was born in Fresno, California, of Korean parents.

Another diver, Mrs. Patricia

CHARLIE CAPOZZOLI

Keller McCormick of Los Angeles, who scored a springboard-platform double in the 1952 Olympics, finished second in the voting with 94 first-place votes and 1,045 points.

Charles Capozzoli of Bayside, the New York A. C.'s rising young distance runner, ranked third with 123 first-place votes and 990 points.

* * *

FOLLOWING IN order were James McLane of Yale University, an outstanding distance swimmer for ten years, with 82 first-place votes and 734 points; Norbert

Schemansky of Detroit, world Olympic and American weight-lifting champion in the middle heavyweight division, 33 first place votes and 345 points and Gail Peters of Washington, D. C., all-around swimmer, 24 first-place votes and 307 points.

Then came J. Lewis (Poppa) Hall, University of Florida high jumper, 20 first-place votes and 303 points, and Mrs. Nancy Cowperthwaite Phillips of New York, a long-time star in women's track and field, eight first-place votes and 206 points.

There were seven write-in first place votes for aMl Whitfield, two-time Olympic 800-meter champion and world record-holder for 880 yards, whose name was not on the official ballot. Wes Santee, 4:02.4 miler from the University of Kansas, received four write-in second-place votes.

Major Lee is cited on the official Sullivan Award ballot as "a courageous competitor, a true sportsman and a man of integrity and high ideals." One of the most popular members of the 1948 and 1952 United States Olympic teams, he won the acclaim of rivals, as well as teammates, for his willingness to help them improve their form. His citation further reads: "The trail of international friends made by Dr. Sammy Lee is as lengthy and encircling as the equator."

CELANESE CORPORATION OF AMERICA

Manufacturers of Celanese *Brand Products*
REG. U. S. PAT. OFF.

290 FERRY STREET   NEWARK 5, NEW JERSEY
TELEPHONE: MITCHELL 2-6800
December 14, 1953

PLASTICS DIVISION

YOUR REF.
OUR REF. JJK-4034-53

Mr. and Mrs. Joseph Capozzoli
163-17 25th Avenue
Flushing, L. I., New York

Dear Mr. and Mrs. Capozzoli:

I was indeed gratified the other day to receive a
letter from the National A. A. U. concerning the 1953 James E. Sullivan
Award for the outstanding amateur athlete, and to note that Charlie was
nominated as one of eight athletes. You need not worry about which
candidate received my vote!

If you have not already seen it, Mary and I felt that
you would like to know a wonderful tribute paid to your son in his nomin-
ation. You may well be proud of bringing up a boy about whom the following
can be said:

"American three mile champion and member of the 1952 United
States Olympic Team. Winner of the three mile run in the
1952 British International Meet in London in which he created
a new American record of 13m. 51.8s. He has represented the
U.S.A. in international competition on several occasions.
Olympic Coach Brutus Hamilton described him as a runner who comes
as close to maximizing his physical potentialities as any runner
he had ever seen. As a student at Georgetown University, from
which he graduated last June, he won many collegiate titles in
middle distance and cross country running.

"He is a deeply religious young man and has been modest in
victory and gracious in defeat. An excellent student, he
plans to continue his studies at Georgetown University for a
career in law. His conduct on and off the track, whether in
practice or competition is impeccable. Unselfish in his
attitude, he has been an inspiration to the many competitors
with whom he has come in contact. A true amateur in every
sense of the word."

Written by "Jack Keville"

Chapter 22
"The Sullivan Award
and the Kevilles"

Jack Keville of Celanese Corporation became a close friend. He attended Georgetown for one year in 1930, 20 years before my time, and then three years at Columbia, graduating in 1934. Jack was a great miler in his day, having run a 4:38 in the early 30's. Like a family member, he encouraged me throughout my track career to do my best. Being an active official at the track meets in Madison Square Garden, he knew some of the greatest runners in the world and would tell me about them. When in Washington, D.C., on business, he would come to Georgetown's campus. We would jog together, discussing how I would run my next race at the garden in New York, and Boston (Boston Knights of Columbus where I ran the 8:55 two-mile).

The Kevilles lived in Scarsdale, New York. Jack and his lovely wife, Mary, would invite me to their home for dinner during the holidays and in-between semesters. Little did I know that sitting across from me at dinner would be his beautiful daughter, Anne. With the elegantly set table, candles flickering, my eyes focused on Anne. I forgot about eating! We had several dates later, but it wasn't in God's plan for us to be more than very close friends, which we are to this day. My wife, Donna, and Anne, became friends. Donna is now in heaven, having passed away December 21, 2001. Anne lives in Florida and I in California. We still communicate and pray for each other.

Not only was Jack Keville an executive with Celanese Corporation, he was also a founder of "The National Plastics Center and Museum" in Leominster, Massachusetts. On Jack's 90th birthday, four years ago, the museum opened and there was a "gala celebration" in his honor for his achievements. A room was named in his honor.

Throughout the years, Jack maintained his physical condition by jogging and walking. He did this up until his mid eighties. When visiting my wife and I here in California, he would excuse himself, put on his track gear, and go for a jog. I wasn't in shape to join him, even though I was 20 years younger. On May 21, 2005, he will celebrate his 94th birthday. God bless you, my dear friend.

"In my heart lie these fond memories, like treasures of gold that one retrieves, of the good times and the bad, the joyful and the sad, I will always remember the Kevilles!"

"Beautiful anne"

MRS. JACK KEVILLE (MARY)

"Mrs. Jack Keville"

Track team captain Jack Keville poses in front o Columbia University Lion.

Chapter 23
"Run For Fun?"

The title of this story is "Run to Win!" However, maybe it should be "Run for Fun!" Isn't that what it's all about?

Nowadays running is more popular than ever. Thousands compete all over the United States in various distance races, the marathon being the most popular. How can it be fun to run "26 miles?" I can't tell you because the longest distance I ever ran was ten miles in Canada, but it wasn't fun. Had thousands been competing as they now do in races ranging from 5K, 10K, and the marathon, I would have enjoyed the "excitement of the crowd."

Once you become too serious about running, or any sport, you may lose the "spirit of enjoyment." Why be upset if you lose a race when you know you did your best? Isn't that what "life" is all about, "doing your best?" Meet and become friends with other participants in the race. Shake hands with them before and after the race. Congratulate one another, regardless how you ended up. Develop lasting friendships. Whether you win or lose, be happy knowing you did your best.

I began running for the fun of it. It was "fun to run" along with others. It later became serious when people expected me to win. This meant training hard everyday and obeying the rules to become a champion. When it came time to "compete and beat" others in the race, it was less fun to run. Run to Win! It's ok, as long as you graciously accept victory, and in the same manner, graciously accept defeat. This builds character, win or lose. You always try harder in your next race, but remember, the person who comes in last in a race may have tried harder than the person who won.

191

Sports build character and prepare you for the big race, "living life!" Life presents many challenges that sports will have prepared you to face. We were amateurs in our day. There was no professionalism back then. Yet we managed to be financially successful, some of us now living in million dollar plus homes. I have many friends, runners, basketball players, etc., who became coaches, doctors, dentists, judges, lawyers, priests, engineers, and executives. What we learned in sports, prepared us for the "challenges of life." There are happy moments in life, there are also sad moments. It's like running a race, you may win one day and lose the next, but you keep on going, "doing your best" and courageously facing the "challenges of life."

How is it possible not waste one minute of your life? Sounds hard and impossible, but every person can do it. From the time you wake up in the morning, offer up everything you do to the one who created you, "God!" When you go to sleep at night, offer up your sleep to Him, "every breath you take, and every movement of your body, and every beat of your heart." You can't go wrong in life by doing this and doing your best

As mentioned in previous chapters, "it's love that really matters." Be on God's team. Then, you can't lose this serious "race of life." It is serious, but the reward is greater than anything we can possibly imagine, greater than winning any other race in life, greater than winning an Olympic title, greater than breaking a world record, and so on.

"Dream of wondrous things, do your best, win or lose, its love that really matters."

Chapter 24
The Last Chapter,
"My Final Race, Yours' Too!"

The start of my "final race of life" began June 19, 1931, when I was born. Everyone's' final race begins when they are born. Each day we are all approaching the finish line; some finish before others.

I "visualize and dream" that I am approaching the finish line. My heart tells me, "don't look back! If you do, remember what happened to "Vefling! Vefling! Vefling!" I can hear the spectators chanting, "Capozzoli! Capozzoli! Capozzoli!" The voices are clear and familiar. They're the voices of my children, grandchildren, and loved ones. They want me to win this final race more than any in my lifetime. There are no other competitors. I'm running alone. I feel the best ever! I've never wanted to win a race as much as this one. I can see the finish line ahead, but there is no tape to break, only crowds of people waiting. I wanted to look back, but my heart said, "No! If you do, you may lose this race!"

As I'm approaching the finish line, the voices rooting for me begin to fade, "go dad, go dad, go grandpa, go grandpa!" "You're near the finish!" "There's the biggest trophy ever waiting for you!"

As their voices fade, I hear other voices at the finish line "Come on Charlie! Come on dad! Come on son! Do your best!" I see faces, my wife's, John's, mom's, dad's, Lou's, Uncle Mike's, grandpa's (champeen of da woild!), aunts, uncles, cousins, friends, Joan's, and "little Marie's." As I cross the finish line, there is only one Angel who was with me all of my life from the very beginning. He carried me across the finish line into the arms of loved ones.

Congratulations came from everyone, George Wright, Frank Sevigne, Brutus Hamilton, Alan Hillman, Al Blozis, Jim fielding, Carl Joyce, Joe La Pierre, and others who already ran and won this "final race of life." I met the other Angels who carried me to victory in past races. They introduced me to the greatest coach of all coaches, yours and mine.

As I said at the beginning of this story, "life passes by so fast, not one minute should be wasted. Dream of wondrous things. It's love that really matters!"

I love you! God Bless!

Your Dad, Grandpa (Papa Charlie) and friend.

"My track shoe dipped
in bronze"

Just prior to graduation, the Georgetown athletic department asked if they could have one of my track shoes. How could I give up one of them that was a big part of me in the many races I ran. They explained, however, that they wanted to dip it in bronze and display it in the future in the trophy room in the lobby of McDonough gymnasium. How could I refuse such an honor?

Some fifty years later, it is still on display. My son, Joe, his wife, Kristie, and five children are shown in the following pictures they took on October 22ⁿᵈ, 2005, when visiting Georgetown with their five children.

My son Joe, his wife, Kristie and five children visited Georgetown University in October, 2005 and took the following pictures in the Trophy Room of the lobby entrance to McDonough Gymnasium.

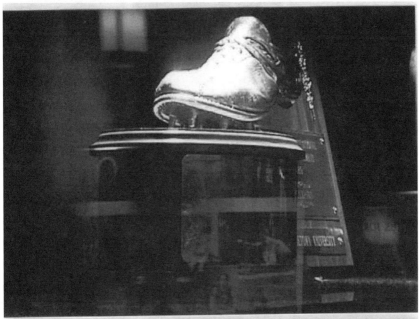

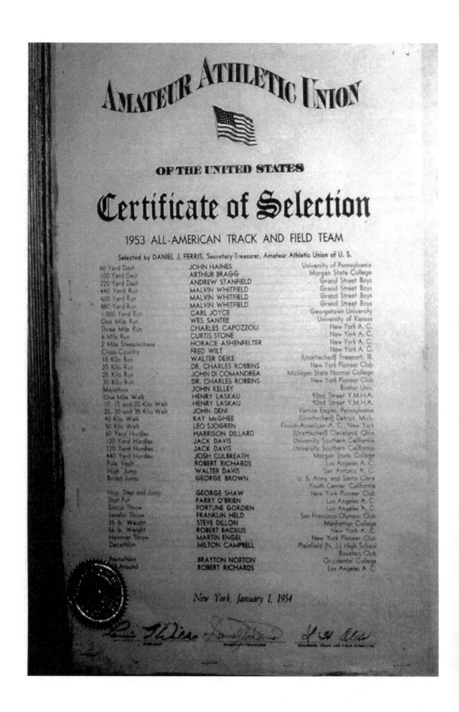

OLYMPIC CIRCLES

The Olympic symbol, recognized throughout the world, consists of five different colored circles on a field of white. Representative of the five continents, these circles are linked together to denote the sporting friendship of the peoples of the earth, whatever their creed or country. The colors of the rings are Blue, Yellow, Black, Green, and Red—colors chosen because at least one of them appears in the flag of every nation in the world. The words "Citius, Altius, Fortius", which frequently appear under the circles, mean "quicker, higher, more strongly", and are indicative of the competing athlete's endeavor to run faster, jump higher, and throw more strongly.

Ex-Olympian keeps fast past 32 years later

It was an Olympic year past, 32 years ago in Helsinki, Finland.

In a tiny, spartan school auditorium near the American team's training camp, head track coach Brutus Hamilton told the group of athletes gathered in front of him, "You have done a tremendous job. You've won all the medals you were supposed to. . .you've won some that you weren't." His voice low and charged with emotion.

Among the elite group on hand was current Monarch Bay resident Charlie Capozzoli, a U.S. distance runner from Flushing, N.Y., often described in those days as a "pair of legs with a big heart."

In a later interview, coach Hamilton would say about the slight 5-feet 8-inch student from Georgetown University, "If I were to mention anyone as being typical of the fine team spirit of this team, it would be Charles Capozzoli. He ran far away the best race of his life."

Today "Cappy," as he was dubbed by sports writers, is Southern California district sales manager for Fender Musical Instruments and a Laguna Niguel resident since 1976. He still remembers his 5,000-meter run at Helsinki.

"I was the fastest of the Americans but I only got seventh in my heat," he recalls. "Only the top five qualified." The highlights of his running career actually came the week after the Olympics during European competition.

"My timing wasn't perfect," he says. "I blossomed a week later and set an American record in the three-mile." Capozzoli won the three-mile in a British Empire vs. USA meet in England. His time of 13:51 was then a record.

"It was a great achievement at that time," he says. "The English were great distance runners."

His pace in the business world today is still fast, according to Capozzoli.

"The musical instrument industry
See CAPPY, page B2

Capozzoli Makes It in Business

Remember Charlie Capozzoli, who came out of Bayside High School to become one of America's brightest running stars at Georgetown University and then did well in the colors of the New York Athletic Club in the 1952 Olympics and other events?

Well, I'm so happy to report, via the good offices of Ed Dahlinger of Forest Hills, long one of Charlie's rooters, that he's made it big, too, in the business world.

He's been appointed national sales manager for CBS Musical Instruments, Fullerton, Calif. and in his new capacity will be responsible for the sales functions of Fender guitars and amplifiers, Rogers drums and Buchla electronic music systems.

Charlie joined CBS/MI in September, 1969, as credit manager . . . in May, 1970, he was named director of marketing, Europe . . . before joining CBS/MI he was with the Richfield Oil Co. and Carte Blanche.

Charlie and his wife, Donna Jane, are the parents of four handsome children and make their home in Santa Ana, Calif. . . . Charlie's parents, Mr. and Mrs. Joseph Capozzoli, still live in Flushing.

John, 16, the oldest of the children has shown no interest in track whatsoever, but I understand that he is quite a high school basketball and baseball player.

CHARLIE CAPOZZOLI

Charlie Capozzoli then . . .   . . . and now

CAPPY: Running strong

From page B1

is very much like athletic competition," he said. "You may be at the top today, but you've got to work your tail off to stay there. The main thing I learned from athletics is to set high goals, make every effort to achieve them and never give up."

In competition, Charlie's dedication, personal effort and unselfish attitude were inspirational to fellow teammates and competitors alike. "I'd always try to go that one extra step beyond what the coach would ask us to do," he says. "It was just the way I had to do things."

Charlie's desire carried him to an IC4A cross country record and a national collegiate cross country record while at Georgetown. Once hailed as America's best bet for the 1956 Olympic distance events, Capozzoli's dreams of gold were altered by a brief military career, marriage and children.

"Those things can have a big impact on your priorities," he said.

Capozzoli actually met his wife at the Coliseum Relays in 1953. They were married two years later.

After stints with Atlantic Richfield and Carte Blanche, Capozzoli joined Fender in 1969.

He is now the father of four children, his youngest, Joseph, a Dana Hills High graduate.

203

OFFICE OF THE
EXECUTIVE SECRETARY

ALUMNI HOUSE

Georgetown University
Alumni Association

3604 O STREET, N.W.
WASHINGTON 7, D. C.

May 29, 1958

Mr. Charles Joseph Capozzoli
915 Conlon Avenue
La Puente, California

Dear Charlie:

  Your name has been placed, in permanent form, on the roster of the Georgetown University Athletic Hall of Fame in the Harbin Trophy Room of McDonough Gymnasium on the Georgetown Campus. The roster contains only the names of the few whom the Athletic Hall of Fame Committee considered the very greatest athletes in Georgetown's long history.

  To formalize the Hall of Fame, a brief ceremony will be held in McDonough Gymnasium on Friday evening, June 6, 1958, at 8:30 P.M. At that time a presentation will be made of a citation attesting to the fact that your name has been selected.

  May I hope that you will be able to be present to receive the citation in person? Please let me know at your convenience that you will be with us. Since the presentation will coincide with the opening of the various class reunions, a large attendance for the presentation is expected.

          Sincerely yours,

          JAMES S. RUBY
          Executive Secretary

205

HOYAS
UNLIMITED

August 14, 1992

Mr. Charles J. Capozzoli
311 Monarch Bay
South Laguna, California 92677

Dear Olympian,

Georgetown University has had its fair share of great athletes, but few have had the honor of being an Olympian. Your participation in the Olympic games symbolizes the very best that one can achieve, and because you are a Hoya we would like to show our appreciation for and celebrate your outstanding accomplishments.

Hoyas Unlimited, in conjunction with the Athletic Department and the Spiked Shoe Club, would like you to be their honored guest at the Hoyas Unlimited Recognition Dinner on October 3, 1992 in the Leavey Center Ballroom at Georgetown University.

Part of the dinner program will be set aside for a tribute to the present and past Georgetown Olympians. A special Olympic plaque will be presented to the athletic department for permanent display, and a video presentation of the 1992 Olympians' performances is expected to be shown. Your name will be inscribed on the plaque and you will receive a miniature replica of the plaque for keepsake.

We hope you will be able to join us. We are expecting over 250 people for the dinner and we are sure that everyone would be honored by your presence.

Sincerely,

Dave Burgess
President, Hoyas Unlimited

Tim Heinle
President, Spiked Shoe Club

P.S. A Complimentary invitation will be forthcoming!

GEORGETOWN UNIVERSITY ALUMNI ASSOCIATION   WASHINGTON, D.C. 20057-1025
202-687-7159

RUN TO WIN

July 15, 1997

Dear Olympian:

We are delighted to enclose a special pin awarded to you by the International
Olympic Committee honoring your participation in the Olympic Games.

These participant lapel pins have been issued under the direction of IOC
President Juan Antonio Samaranch to be presented to every Olympic Team
member worldwide. The United States customarily fields the largest number
of Olympic competitors for each team and has had more total participants
than any other country dating back to 1896. The U.S. Olympic Committee is
very proud of this historical tradition and we are indebted to you for your
athletic contribution.

On behalf of the U.S. Olympic Family, we extend our best wishes and
congratulations.

Sincerely,

WILLIAM J. HYBL
President

RICHARD D. SCHULTZ
Executive Director

Enclosure

United States Olympic Committee
One Olympic Plaza
Colorado Springs, Colorado 80909
Tel: 719-632-5551

Charlie Capozzoli

July 15, 1997

Dear Olympian:

We are delighted to enclose a special pin awarded to you by the International Olympic Committee honoring your participation in the Olympic Games.

These participant lapel pins have been issued under the direction of IOC President Juan Antonio Samaranch to be presented to every Olympic Team member worldwide. The United States customarily fields the largest number of Olympic competitors for each team and has had more total participants than any other country dating back to 1896. The U.S. Olympic Committee is very proud of this historical tradition and we are indebted to you for your athletic contribution.

On behalf of the U.S. Olympic Family, we extend our best wishes and congratulations.

Sincerely,

WILLIAM J. HYBL
President

RICHARD D. SCHULTZ
Executive Director

Enclosure

United States Olympic Committee
One Olympic Plaza
Colorado Springs, Colorado 80909
Tel: 719-632-5551

The Coca-Cola Company

COCA-COLA PLAZA
ATLANTA, GEORGIA

DONALD R. KNAUSS
PRESIDENT AND CHIEF OPERATING OFFICER
COCA-COLA NORTH AMERICA

ADDRESS REPLY TO
P. O. BOX 1734
ATLANTA, GA 30301

404 676-0700
FAX: 404 515-0010

December 27, 2005

Dear U.S. Olympic Alumni,

The Coca-Cola Company has been committed to the Olympic Movement since the 1928 Olympic Games in Amsterdam. This year, we are particularly excited about our U.S. Olympic promotional program which includes a $1 million donation from The Coca-Cola Company in support of Team USA. I thought we should share that news along with the rest of our plan with you, our United States Olympians.

The over-arching theme for all of our Company's international efforts around the Torino Olympic Winter Games will be "Live Olympic." A call to action, Live Olympic speaks to all of us--athletes, spectators and sponsors. It asks the question: What if we embraced the spirit of the Olympic Games every two seconds instead of every two years?

The Live Olympic campaign, which will be activated globally by The Coca-Cola Company, will be adapted specifically for the North American market. Just as Live Olympic asks us all to aspire to the Olympic Ideal, it calls on The Coca-Cola Company to commit its resources to U.S. Olympic excellence. Therefore, a critical feature of the Coca-Cola North America effort—one that will be of particular interest to U.S. Olympians, U.S. Olympic hopefuls in training and their coaches--is the $1 million dollar donation from The Coca-Cola Company to Team USA.

The power of our Live Olympic messaging and the renewed focus on the athlete will be reinforced by the direct involvement of the following members of TEAM USA: Michelle Kwan, Apolo Anton Ohno, Vonetta Flowers, Joe Pack, and Paralympian Ralph Green. They will be featured in the Company's Olympic-related advertising and marketing.

For me, the most profound element of our approach to the 2006 Olympic Winter Games is the focus on the U.S. Olympic Team. The five athletes listed above reflect the dynamism and drive of the entire United States Olympic and Paralympic Teams, as well as the diversity of America's hopes in Torino.

These athletes, like you and all U.S. Olympians, represent the very best of "living Olympic." Your devotion to the Olympic Ideal inspires us, in fact you can see that it forms the core of our 2006 plan. As a small token of our appreciation for your inspiration of the Company's efforts and out of respect for your Olympic accomplishments, we have enclosed a limited edition "Live Olympic" T-Shirt as well as a "Live Olympic" automobile window sticker. We hope you will enjoy these gifts and sport them with pride as you join The Coca-Cola Company in cheering on the United States in Torino.

Thank you for your inspiration.

Sincerely,

Donald R. Knauss
President

"Our Wedding Day,
January 2nd, 1955"

Following are pictures of our wedding day. Donna and I were Married at St. Thomas Catholic Church in Los Angeles (City of the Angels!) One picture is with Donna and her bridesmaids. Note: Joan and Betty whom I am sure you can pick out from their Graduation pictures shown in a prior chapter, "California here We come!" Two of Donna's sisters, Barbara and Joyce, and Cousins also appear. Her sister, Pat, wasn't in the wedding Party, since she was pregnant at the time. Donna's parents, Dante and Frieda Dente, are shown along with Donna and me, The "lucky salesman" from New York and "runner" from Georgetown University. I won the grand prize, "Donna Dente, The girl of my dreams!"

Unfortunately, my parents, living in New York weren't able to attend. A picture of my parents on their wedding day appears at the beginning of this story. I wasn't able to attend their wedding either (wasn't born yet).

"Dream of wondrous things!" "Dreams do come true!" "It's love and family that really matters!" "God first, family next!"

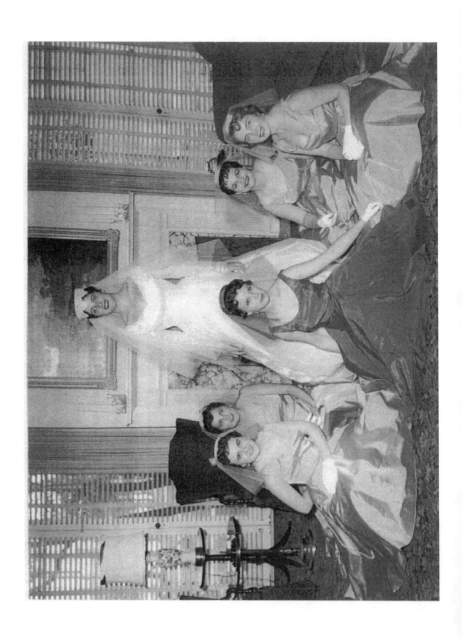

"Our Son John"

"Oct. 24th, 1955 – Sept. 2nd, 2005"

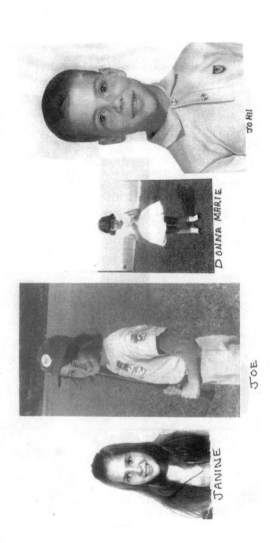

"John Capozzoli's Three Miracles!"
Written By His Father

"His first miracle!"

When John was eight years old, he had cancer and was given six months to live. Two surgeries took place, the first being several weeks before "Christmas," the second being on "Good Friday." The surgeon said that John had a rare cancer that would attack his nervous system and spread throughout his body. It had spread to his lymph nodes. The doctor said nothing more could be done.

"We can pray," his parents politely replied.

His parents asked God to spare his life if it was for the benefit of his soul and the souls of others. It was their desire to see him grow up, fall in love, marry, and have children of his own.

Loved ones, friends, and people who never met or knew John prayed for him. In desperation, his parents wrote a letter to "Pope Pius VI." It was delivered to him by a Jesuit friend of the family, Father Daley, who happened to be in Rome at the time. A reply was received from the Secretariat to the Pope advising John's parents that the Pope was praying for him. He enclosed a Rosary with a relic.

From the time his parents were told that the Pope was praying for him, John's health improved. Many visits were made to the doctor until there were no more signs of the cancer. Finally no more visits were required. His parents watched him grow up, fall in love, with a beautiful lady, named Pamela, and have two children of his own, Annalisa and Andrea. He now had the family that his parents prayed for.

"John's second miracle!"

Many years later, John's mother came down with Ovarian Cancer and passed away December 21, 2001. She was 65 years old. John spoke of "love" at her funeral mass. A year and a half later, John, then forty-eight years old, was diagnosed as having cancer of the stomach and esophagus. Surgery immediately took place, his stomach being removed and part of his esophagus. The remaining esophagus was attached to his colon. Again, the surgeon gave him three to six months to live, since 15% of the cancer remained in him that could not be removed. It was near the aorta, hard as concrete, and would take a hammer and chisel to remove it.

Life changed for John and his family. He was bedridden and fed formula through his tummy. He received communion daily in a normal manner. After one year, he told his wife he wanted to go to "Lourdes" where the "Blessed Virgin Mary" appeared and many miracles took place.

Off they went at the generosity of "the Knights of Malta." John took his formula and feeding tube with him, boarded the plane in a wheelchair and returned home walking on his own. His health improved, but the feeding tube and remaining cancer was still in him. It was decided by another surgeon to operate and remove the remaining cancer, estimated hours of surgery being four hours or longer. After three hours of surgery, the surgeon removed the feeding tube, stitched the wound, and rushed to tell the good news to his wife, "I could find no cancer in him! He's cancer free!"

His wife and father shed many tears of happiness. Another miracle, the second, had taken place!

John began to live a normal life, eating, walking, cooking, and diving for lobster, one of his favorite sports. We enjoyed the lobster, but more important, it was because John caught them. Several months later, the Oncologist wanted to follow up on his health by doing a Pet Scan and Cat Scan. The report came in.

John said to his dad, "I lit up like a Christmas tree," meaning the cancer showed up in other parts of his body. Radiation and chemo treatments immediately began... It meant long trips from Dana Point to Los Angeles for John and his wife. John's energy level faded and it became difficult for him to eat, but yet he looked forward to daily Holy Communion that he was able to receive in a normal manner. Things got worse before they got better, but John never complained, only apologizing to his wife and father for being a burden. Two more surgeries took place.

"The third and final miracle,
the miracle of all miracles!"

John could no longer eat, experiencing great pain, but never complaining, only apologizing. He would call his father around ten in the evening saying,

"Dad! Thank you for bringing me Communion."

"I love bringing you Communion. Someday you'll do it for me." he replied.

"I love you Dad."

"I love you John!"

John's weight began to drop rapidly. He spent most time in bed, eating very little, getting up late in the evening to sit on the patio at his favorite spot in his new home. He told his father how much he enjoyed the evenings and would sit there until two or three in the morning, many times calling his sister, Donna Marie, who would listen to him for hours. She knew he needed her attention. His wife was exhausted and needed rest to continue the care he required throughout the day and until the late evenings.

Once again, the doctors told John they could do no more for him and that he had two weeks to two months to live. We all knew it was time for the third miracle, the time for John to be with the one who loved him more than anyone, his Creator. God heard our prayers when the first miracle took place forty years ago. John met his lovely wife, and had the family we prayed for him to have. The second miracle took place at Lourdes. Now was the time for John to be rewarded for his patient suffering in carrying the cross, which was his and his alone.

John and his wife planned his funeral knowing there wasn't much time left.

"I want a simple casket," he requested. "a pine box, and want to be dressed in an Alb, a white linen garment similar to a robe. I want you to have a big party after I die. I wonder how many people will be at my funeral?"

During his final days, John's wife, his two daughters, his father, his sisters, brother, aunts, uncles, nieces, nephews, and friends surrounded him with love. Echoing throughout his home you could hear, "I love you! We love you, John!"

Five priests visited him during his last two weeks, spending hours with him, his wife, and children. In spite of his suffering, John managed to meet his visitors and would say to them, "I love you!"

He received Communion except for the day before he died when he was unable to open his mouth. He could no longer speak. We spoke to him. "I love you, John! We love you, John!"

A few hours before he died in his loving wife's arms, he said his last three words to her, "I saw heaven!"

This was his third and final miracle!

The Rosary took place several days later, the funeral the following day. The church was crowded to capacity, people sitting up in the balcony. Many spoke of the love that John had for them, his wife, his children, his mother and father, his sisters, brother, relatives, and friends. The gospel read by father Pat Brennan, who accompanied John and the Knights of Malta to Lourdes, was as follows:

"Whoever eats this bread will live forever, and I will raise them up on the last day."

(John 6:51-59)

After the funeral mass, a big party (reception) took place at Knight Hall and again later at his home, after the burial at Ascension Cemetery, near his mother. His four wishes came true.

"We thank you God for the precious gift you gave us, John Capozzoli!"

In Loving Memory of
John Capozzoli
October 24, 1955 – September 2, 2005

LOVE

Such a wonderful word that in the midst of trails and tribulations it overwhelms us with it's peace. It' guides through the most terrific times that we have and renders us harmless in the tough times and in our sorrows. This Love won't ever be conquered. Love is endless and very forgiving. It knows no bounds and only knows to seek out and dispense. O how I wish we could convert to this gracious love. What mankind could experience would be a total freedom and the taste of Heaven. A reality that could definetly bring man to the doorstep to Heaven.

Love is not giddish, foolish, follical, Love is strong it forgives, surrounds you with great and immense power. Do not underestimate this Love. It will pick you from the deepest depth"s and embrace you with such force the sheer experience can make you cry tears of joy.

Love does not boast , is kind, gentle, and is not revengeful, jeaulous, spiteful or impatient. This love only knows how to sacrifice with no bounds O what a wonderful love to have in our grasps. Pray this love enwarmth's you so that you may have a peace not known to man and the same time shatter satin's plan to rob us of this most precious gift given to us by OUR SAVIOUR JESUS CHRIST.

How beautiful to live in this love, it's like an all encompassing shroud covering you with warmth and peace beyond all means. To have this love within us it's guides us to the most of all peaceful places in the aura of heaven. Only fools wouldn't want this love!

11/7 2002 C Capt

Presented by my son, John, to his wife, Pamela, on their 16th Wedding Anniversary, several months after their return from "Lourdes!"

ABOVE: STATUE NOW IN JOHN AND PAM'S YARD
BOUGHT BY HIS PARENTS WHEN HE WAS EIGHT YEARS
OLD.

BELOW: JOHN AND PAM IN LOURDES

ABOVE AND BELOW: JOHN AND PAM HAPPILY
TOGETHER, THE THREE OF THEM, JOHN, PAM,
AND "OUR LADY OF LOURDES."

ABOVE: JOHN ENCLOSED IN HIS CART IN LOURDES.

BELOW: JOHN BEING USHERED AROUND BY THE CARING AND LOVING "KNIGHTS OF MALTA."

ABOVE AND BELOW: JOHN IS SAFE AND SOUND WITH
HIS LOVING WIFE AT HIS SIDE, HIS HEAVENLY MOTHER,
"OUR LADY OF LOURDES," WATCHING OVER HIM, AND
HIS MOTHER, DONNA, BEAMING DOWN AT HER SON.

PICTURE OF JOHN TAKEN IN HIS YARD TWO MONTHS AFTER HIS ARRIVAL HOME FROM LOURDES AND WHEN THE FEEDING TUBE WAS REMOVED FROM HIS TUMMY

SAFELY HOME

I am home in Heaven, dear ones;
  Oh, so happy and so bright!
There is perfect joy and beauty
  In this everlasting light.

All the pain and grief is over,
  Every restless tossing passed;
I am now at peace forever,
  Safely home in Heaven at last.

Did you wonder I so calmly
  Trod the valley of the shade?
Oh! but Jesus' love illumined
  Every dark and fearful glade.

And He came Himself to meet me
  In that way so hard to tread;
And with Jesus' arm to lean on,
  Could I have one doubt or dread?

Then you must not grieve so sorely,
  For I love you dearly still:
Try to look beyond earth's shadows,
  Pray to trust our Father's Will.

There is work still waiting for you,
  So you must not idly stand;
Do it now, while life remaineth—
  You shall rest in Jesus' land.

When that work is all completed,
  He will gently call you Home;
Oh, the rapture of that meeting,
  Oh, the joy to see you come!

"My Baby's Song"

Go to sleep my baby,
Dream of wondrous things,
For today is all over,
And who knows what tomorrow brings

It's love that really matters,
And in our heart it sings,
So dream my darling baby,
For who knows what tomorrow brings,

When you are awaken,
Your dreams will seem so real,
You'll wish they weren't taken,
For you'll know just how it feels,

So.... Dream my darling baby
Dream of wondrous things,
For today will soon be over,
And who knows what tomorrow brings.

And now it is tomorow,
Your dreams have all come true,
They'll be no tears or sorrrow,
There's only joy for you

So.... Dream my darling baby
Dream of wondrous things,
For today will soon be over,
And who knows what tomorrow brings.

231

"CHARLIE, MARION, LOU"

"MOM & DAD"

COLLEGE GRADUATION PARTY 1953

TREASURES OF GOLD

BY CHARLIE CAPOZZOLI
311 MONARCH BAY
SO. LAGUNA, CA. 9262
(714) 499-4752

AS A CHILD............I REMEMBER MOM AND DAD,
ALL THE FUN...THE GOOD TIMES AND THE SAD,
THE LOVE THEY GAVE..THE SACRIFICES MADE,
I WILL ALWAYS REMEMBER........MOM AND DAD,

IN MY HEART..............LIE THESE FOND MEMORIES,
LIKE TREASURES OF GOLD THAT ONE RETRIEVES
..................OF THE THE GOOD TIMES AND THE BAD
.............................THE JOYFUL AND THE SAD,
ARE THE MEMORIES OF..............MY MOM AND DAD,

IN THE MORNING...............WHEN WE WOULD ARISE,
IN THE EVENING.....BEFORE WE CLOSED OUR EYES,
THERE WAS A HUG AND A KISS.............................
A LOT OF HAPPINESS...
I WILL ALWAYS REMEMBER............MOM AND DAD.....

ALTHOUGH............... WE ARE NOW FAR APART,
THEIR LOVE..............LINGERS ON IN MY HEART,
..................THE STORIES...................I'VE TOLD,
..................ARE LIKE......... TREASURES OF GOLD,
BURIED.....DEEP.......DEEP........WITHIN MY HEART,

.......AND NOW MY CHILD.................YOU CAN TELL,
THE SAME STORIES AS WELL.................................
OF THE LOVE WE GAVE....THE SACRIFICES MADE,
MAY YOU ALWAYS REMEMBER.....MOM AND DAD,
.....I WILL ALWAYS REMEMBER.........MOM AND DAD,

"The Capozzoli Family."

The center picture was taken at our annual cookout at the beach . All of our relatives and friends attended. Joe, in the center, took charge of the cooking with his mother and brother at his side helping him. This was the beginning of Joe's becoming a great chef and now owner of the famous "Capozzoli's Pizzeria and Restaurant' in Oceanside, California.

DONNA MARIE + DAD (GODFATHER)

JANINE

DONNA MARIE

DAD, MOM, JOHN, JOE, JANINE, DONNA MARIE

The annual cookout no longer takes place since the passing of my wife Donna, and our son, John. However, Joe and his wife, Kristie, have made sure they are always with us at the restaurant by prominently displaying pictures of them for all to admire.

Below are pictures of Janine and Joe in their younger days. Janine, Donna Marie, myself, and other family members, enjoy assisting Joe and Kristie at their famous "Capozzoli's Pizzeria and Restaurant." It's a happy and fun place with wonderful ambience and delicious food. "It's love that really matters!"

JANINE

JOE

My Adopted Family

Semper Fi

Sir,

I wanted to send you and your family a small token of appreciation for your support not only of me, but of so many marines. It means a lot to my marines and I to know folks back home care, and you show it on a day to day basis which is truly appreciated.

I look forward to seeing you and enjoying Capozzoli's restaurant upon my return from Iraq. Semper Fidelis,
Beau

This certificate of appreciation
Was prepared onboard
U.S. Marine Corps Base

Camp Fallujah, Iraq

In Recognition of the great support from

Charlie Capozzoli and The Friends and Family of

Capozzoli's Restaurant

on this

15th day of August 2007
during

Operation Iraqi Freedom 06 – 08.2

Lieutenant Colonel Beau Higgins, USMC
Commanding Officer, 1st Reconnaissance Battalion

Sergeant Major A. D. Miller, USMC
Sergeant Major, 1st Reconnaissance Battalion

SILENT
SWIFT
DEADLY
1st RECON BN.

To: The Capozzoli's

From: MGySgt Russ Pankievich and the 3rd LAR Maintenance Team in Mudaysis, Iraq

Thanks for taking care of my family while I'm away! I'm looking forward to getting back for a good glass of wine, a terrific dinner and some time to catch up with my friends!

Semper Fi,

Russ

The Saga of a Maverick Leatherneck
from Cadet to Marine Lt. Colonel

Neil Levin

I wrote this book to Julia Ann and Christopher, my grandson. Julia Ann told her mother she already knew all about my flying adventures such as me being shot down.

"Julia, how could you know about what happened to Pop Pop?" Donna asked.

"Mother, before I was born I was an Angel in Heaven and I used to look down and I could see my Pop Pop. I watched him flying. I watched him get shot down and I watched his men coming to get him. There were some bad men coming to get him too. I watched to make sure his men got to him before the bad men did."

When I heard this, I got teary eyed. Of course, the child probably listened to my stories and then again, maybe not. I like to think she was the Angel that protected me.

As I look back at the many times I have somehow managed to survive extreme danger and life threatening situations during my twenty-year military flying career, I must admit one thing.

I do believe an Angel Rode My Wing.

"AN ANGEL RODE MY WING, BY LT. COL. NEIL LEVIN!"

A true story about a great person who served his country as a Marine Pilot during the Vietnam war and afterwards. It is excellent reading for all.

This life story is truly inspiring, especially for our men and women in the military, and for those who are contemplating to serve our country.

This story tells what it takes to be a true servant for ones' country and the values which make America what it is today, "A land of freedom, a place to enjoy life!"

"The Capozzoli Family" are very proud of you, Lt. Col. Neil Levin. We are proud of all our military, Marines, Army, Navy, Air Force, Coast Guard, men and women alike, for the sacrifices you and your family make. It is because of you that our country is great, "the land of the free and of the brave!" May God Bless You.

To order "An Angel Rode My Wing" by Lt. Col. Neil Levin, a true story, please call (760) 967-9575, or go to www.leatherneckpublishing.com

ABOUT THE AUTHOR

Charlie Capozzoli challenges any finish line in all aspects of his life. He grew up in a close, loving Italian family with impeccable integrity, morals and work ethics. He worked for his father (his inspiration) as a youth until he left home at 18 years for Georgetown University. Since he didn't know much about his grandfather or great grandfather, Charlie wrote this book to leave something significant for his grandchildren.

Today in retirement, he spends his weekends as the iconic host at his son's famous Italian restaurant, "Capozzoli's Pizzeria & Restaurant" in Oceanside, California.

To order this book, please visit:
www.charliecapozzoli.com